Forecasting Political Events

Forecasting Political Events
The Future of Hong Kong

Bruce Bueno de Mesquita
David Newman
Alvin Rabushka

Yale University Press
NEW HAVEN AND LONDON

This book is dedicated, as we are, to
ARLENE
CHRISTINE
AND
LOUISA

Published with the assistance of the A. Whitney Griswold Publication Fund.

Designed by James J. Johnson and set in Times Roman type.
Printed in the United States of America by Edwards Brothers Inc., Ann Arbor, Michigan.

Library of Congress Cataloging in Publication Data

Bueno de Mesquita, Bruce, 1946–
  Forecasting political events.

  Includes bibliographical references and index.
  1. Hong Kong—Politics and government. I. Newman,
David, 1956–   . II. Rabushka, Alvin. III. Title.
DS796.H757B84 1985   951'.2505   85–8166
ISBN 0–300–03519–5 (alk. paper)

The paper in this book meets the guidelines for permanence and durability of the Committee on Production Guidelines for Book Longevity of the Council on Library Resources.

10 9 8 7 6 5 4 3 2 1

Contents

v

7777

Preface

On September 26, 1984, the governments of Great Britain and the People's Republic of China initialed a draft agreement by which Britain agreed to transfer sovereignty and administrative authority over Hong Kong to China on July 1, 1997. China, in turn, has promised to maintain Hong Kong's free-wheeling capitalistic economic system and other liberties for at least fifty years after 1997. China's current intentions are sincere, but Hong Kong's residents—investors, workers, intellectuals, civil servants, and expatriates—must try to determine for themselves how durable China's promises will be. China's flip-flops over its own economic policies during the past three decades make Hong Kong investors and residents uneasy about the prospect that China will steadfastly honor its guarantees over the long run. The issue is therefore the durability, not the short-run credibility, of China's written word. This is the central policy question addressed in this book: Can China be counted on to enforce the terms of the Joint Declaration on the future of Hong Kong?

Although both sides sought to preserve the stability and prosperity of Hong Kong both in the transition years to 1997 and beyond, a host of key questions required resolution. Included among the central economic issues are ownership of property, free movement of labor, capital, unrestricted travel, the right of trade in any currency, retention of Hong Kong's free-port status, maintenance of an independent, fully convertible currency backed by external assets, terms of land-lease renewals, the scope of social welfare programs, regulation of labor, and local tax policy. Legal and political issues include the structure of government, selection of the chief executive, election of members to the local legislature, independence of the judiciary from Beijing, the rights of individuals under the common law, and freedom of speech, press, assembly, education, marriage, and family. Other issues involve Hong Kong's links with countries that have no diplomatic relations with China and the continued existence of Nationalist Chinese activities in Hong Kong after 1997. Concerns over China's policies following its resumption of sovereignty were eloquently expressed by a delegation of appointed local Hong Kong officials who visited London during debate on the Hong Kong question in the British House of Commons. The crux of their worries appeared in a statement highlighting vast differences between communist China and Hong Kong: "The inescapable fact is that the Chinese government is committed to a political philosophy which is at least incompatible, and at worst hostile, to the philosophy on which the various systems and freedoms enjoyed by Hong Kong today rest."

This book addresses the question of the scope and durability of China's future policies toward Hong Kong through the application of a formal interest group theory of politics that explains the process by which policy decisions are made and predicts specifically the resolution of the concrete issues that comprise the agenda for collective choice. The theory elaborated in chapter 2 is an expected utility model of decision making that builds upon earlier work by Bruce Bueno de Mesquita, outlined in his book *The War Trap* and in subsequent journal articles. The model represents a rigorous method of studying politics that seeks to analyze the policy choices reached, to identify the political realignments that may result from a forecasted policy decision and the implications of these new alignments, and to evaluate the significance of alternative assumptions in order to assess the degree of confidence that can be placed in derived policy forecasts. It is a parsimonious model that requires only data on the relevant political actors who seek to influence policy, the policy preference of each actor arrayed on the possible policy continuum, estimates of the relevant capabilities of each group, and the salience each group attaches to each issue. These data are readily available from experts who study given countries or substantive issues.

We have arrayed this theory against the issue of the future of Hong Kong, making precise forecasts on more than a dozen concrete issues that will determine Hong Kong's post-1997 economic, political, legal, and social systems. There are three sets of analyses. The first analysis, of the structure and contents of the Sino—British accord, was completed in March 1984, so we can compare our forecasts with the actual terms of the agreement announced in September 1984, some six months later. Using the same analytical tool, we completed the second and third analyses in the summer of 1984, forecasting changes within Hong Kong between 1985 and 1997, before China recovers the colony, and post-1997 policies in Hong Kong under Chinese sovereignty and administrative authority that will reflect the political dynamics inside China. Each is a real-time forecast. Those who suspect that our accuracy in forecasting the terms of the 1984 accord was purely fortuitous can reserve judgment and compare our post-1984 predictions with events as they unfold.

We have lots of organizations and people to thank. The March 1984 analysis was completed as a commercial project by a joint venture between Data Resources, Inc., and Policon Corporation for several commercial clients. It was released as a formal document in March 1984, thus affirming our claim of its completion six months in advance of the negotiated joint declaration between Britain and China. We thank Data Resources, Inc., and Policon Corporation for permission to use the data collected for that report and for the use of Data Resources' computers, on which all the analyses for this study were completed. Among the key individuals at Data Resources to whom we are indebted are Douglas Beck, Christa Dub, and Laura Krouse.

Several people read various portions of the manuscript. For their comments we thank Kenneth Organski, Jacek Kugler, and Elizabeth Jones and Marian Ash, our always helpful editors at Yale University Press.

Money is a crucial ingredient in modern social science. Bruce Bueno de Mesquita thanks the University of Rochester for travel support that financed final revisions. He also thanks the Scaife Family Charitable Trusts and the Hoover Institution for grants that supported the project. David Newman thanks the Hoover Institution Publications Committee for a travel grant that enabled him to complete work on the first draft. Alvin Rabushka thanks the Hoover Institution for its financial support and outstanding facilities, which made his work on this book possible.

We thank our experts who supplied the data inputs for the expected utility model. Without their expertise, the abstract logic in the model could not have generated concrete forecasts. Apart from the formal experts, we thank George W. Huntley for additional insights he supplied on the dynamics and motives of both sides in the Sino-British negotiations on the future of Hong Kong. Louisa A. Rabushka typed a portion of the manuscript at her husband's urging. Janice Brown and Helaine McMenomy provided invaluable assistance in preparing the manuscript. Yale University Press provided excellent support at every step in the publishing process.

We gratefully acknowledge the help we received from all these sources, who are, of course, not responsible for any errors, shortcomings, or conclusions in our book. In any multiauthored work, errors of fact or interpretation are the fault of the other guys.

1
Thinking about Politics

Since the time of the ancient Greeks, man has observed, thought about, and analyzed politics. A litany of famous political thinkers—all household names—includes Plato, Aristotle, Cicero, Aquinas, Machiavelli, Hobbes, Locke, Rousseau, Jefferson, and Marx, to name a few. These men, and hundreds like them over the centuries, have explored a broad range of normative, scientific, and, most recently, policy objectives. Political philosophers have examined moral, ethical, and value judgments in trying to prescribe the ideal political system, justice, and the true goals of politics. Political scientists have tried to develop theories that can be used to explain and predict how people will behave in the empirical world. They have developed an incredible variety of conceptual, mathematical, statistical, and other research techniques in the quest for a science of politics. Most recently, the burgeoning field of policy analysis has emerged. Its practitioners have tried to marry an understanding of politics with the pursuit of specific policy objectives.

Every student of politics is familiar with the distinction between facts and values, between the *is* and the *ought*. Scientific statements are based upon evidence about the world of experience; they are verified as true or rejected as false through empirical testing. Normative statements, in contrast, are neither

1

true nor false. They are value judgments that no amount of empirical evidence can prove or disprove. To take but one example, a political scientist can study how reforming the federal income tax alters the behavior of special interest groups, but it takes individual value judgments to determine whether a change in the incidence of the tax burden is desirable.

WHAT IS POLITICS?

Perhaps a useful way to answer this question is to contrast politics with economics. The science of economics is concerned with the allocation of scarce resources in a society. Scarcity implies that choices must be made among alternative uses of any one resource. Choice, in turn, entails costs—the money one uses to buy railway equipment cannot be used to purchase jet aircraft. The resources available to people determine how much and what mix of goods and services they can feasibly produce. Of course, it makes sense to produce as much as possible at the least possible cost, which means that there are more goods and services to go around and more people can afford them—a common-sense notion of economic efficiency.

A market is a place or device enabling people to negotiate exchanges. In the marketplace, individuals compare their personal valuations as they buy or sell goods and services. Buyers and sellers conclude their exchanges after settling on a price, which is typically expressed in the units of some currency. In the modern electronic age, markets can range in scope from the Sunday morning village bazaar to the interconnected twenty-four-hour gold markets in New York, London, Zurich, and Hong Kong, in which buyers and sellers throughout the world can negotiate exchanges at a single price.

Let us define the market mechanism more precisely. The market is a method of organization in which owners of property and labor services make individual decisions to produce, distribute, and consume on the basis of unregulated prices. In a free market economy, a simplified model employed by economists, the government does not interfere with the prices established by market forces—the supply and demand conditions resulting from millions of individual decisions to buy and sell—nor does it protect existing firms from the pressure of competitors. Resources are free to move: new producers are allowed to compete with existing ones, and existing producers are allowed to go out of business if they wish.

Put another way, market transactions are voluntary exchanges between buyers and sellers. Markets not only allow each person to exchange the goods and services he produces for those he wants, they also allocate resources for the society as a whole. People interacting in markets determine what products and services are provided within a society, how much of each is produced, what price is attached to each item, and so forth. So long as free entry and unregulated prices prevail, every individual transaction represents a *voluntary* and *unanimous* agreement between the parties to the exchange. Although we think of economic activity as competition among producers for the attention of consumers, cooperation is the defining characteristic of the final agreement between buyer and seller.

Of course, the real world of markets is not so simple. Somebody has to define property rights, enforce contracts, protect people from fraud—in short, establish and enforce the rules of the economic game. The responsibility for these tasks falls upon government. In addition, the rationale for government can arise purely in economic terms. Often the conditions of the free market are not satisfied. The presence of monopolies (the absence of competition), external factors (e.g., pollution) which inflict costs that are not compensated, and the need to provide such public goods as defense (because private suppliers have no practical way to charge for such services) are all examples of economic conditions that call for governmental intervention. Apart from these economic tasks, many also want to accomplish various social and political purposes through the medium of government—advancing education, imposing religious values, preventing abortion, signing international agreements, and so on. These activities cost money and often force people to behave in ways they would otherwise not behave. Only government, with its legal monopoly on coercion, has the power to tax and regulate to attain these objectives.

It makes sense, then, to define one aspect of politics as the study of governmental decision making. Government is the legally based institutions of a society that make legally binding decisions. Governments possess a legal monopoly on the use of coercion, which may be employed to force recalcitrant citizens into line. In the market, all exchanges are based on voluntary consent and no consumer can be forced to part with his money against his will. A distinguishing feature of politics is its coercive nature: citizens can be forced to act against their will.

But equating politics with government is too narrow. The study of politics more generally encompasses the study of power, authority, and conflict. Politics is found wherever power relationships or conflict situations exist—activities that are not resolvable through voluntary market exchanges. In other words, political decisions are nonmarket decisions. Coercion replaces voluntariness, and some decision rule, ranging from dictatorship to majority rule, replaces unanimity. Underpinning the concepts of conflict and power is the idea of people or groups trying to influence the behavior of others and the outcomes of decisions that affect society. Examples range from such nongovernmental issues as tenure decisions in academia or the selection of political party candidates and platforms to such specific governmental decisions as the adoption of a national language or religion, retirement pensions for the elderly, publicly financed health care, how many missiles to buy, what alliances to form with other nations, and whether to alleviate poverty by using the taxing power of the state to redistribute income, to name a few. Political decisions are authoritative for a given social milieu, from a club to an entire nation; they are binding on all members, even those who dislike the results and may have to bear the costs. In brief, politics has to do with the use of power, frequently through institutions of governments, to resolve or settle conflicts over social values and the distribution of public goods.

Let us recapitulate the main differences between markets and politics. In the marketplace, costs and benefits are largely individual affairs. People are rewarded on the basis of their productivity and the return on their investments. The key aspects of market exchange are voluntariness and unanimity. No individual is forced to buy something she does not wish to buy. Political choice, in contrast, entails a group decision, such as majority vote. The group agreement required in political decisions narrows individual choice. Political competition requires individuals to group themselves into coalitions; markets do not. In addition, under all less than unanimous decisions, some portion of the population will have views enforced upon it that are not its own. Although some economic entities may have enormous wealth and power, the most effective power is that which can be enforced by the police power of government. In short, economics involves the cooperation of buyer and seller, whereas politics entails conflict among individuals and groups over the social use of material things or values.

Politics can be defined as the process within or between political communities whereby individuals, groups, or nations struggle for power to advance their own interests and desires. Politics can also be defined as *outcome oriented*, involving the resolution of issues by means of authoritative actions taken on public problems. A comprehensive study of political activity must incorporate both the processes leading to conflict resolution and the outcomes that follow. The ingredients of political investigation include participants, resources, values, governmental institutions, decision-making rules, the adoption of specific policies, and the implementation, evaluation, and subsequent modification of those policies. Political scientists have specialized in the study of political culture, political parties, public opinion, elections and voting behavior, interest groups, the formal institutions (legislative, executive, and judicial) of government, levels of government (local, state, national, and international), public administration, and, most recently, public policy. They have undertaken these studies in the context of the American political system, in the course of comparative analyses across nations, and in the relations among nations. In the course of these investigations, they have used a variety of conceptual frameworks, including systems analysis, structural functional analysis, communications theory, decision making theory, rational choice and game theory, simulation, individual psychological approaches (personality, socialization, learning), small group analysis, Marxism, elitist and pluralist conceptions of the distribution of power, cost–benefit analysis, role theory, and so forth.

THE OBJECTIVES OF POLITICAL SCIENCE

This book develops and tests a formal interest group theory of politics. The theory explains the process of conflict resolution among important individuals and groups over a broad range of issues and predicts or forecasts the results of that process. It is, therefore, both *process* and *outcome oriented*. The theory specifies precisely what information is needed to perform the analysis. It is, we believe, a framework that all students of political analysis and policy forecasting can use for a large menu of domestic and international questions. Maintaining the distinction between *is* and *ought*, the theory does not try to determine "desirable" policy outcomes. However, it can aid participants in the policy process in developing strategies to enhance their positions.

The twin objectives of science are explanation and prediction. Political science seeks to explain why people behave politically as they do, why political processes and institutions function as they do, and why specific outcomes occur. The logical structures of explanation and prediction are the same; the difference between them is only whether the scientist's objective is to account for a past event or describe a future event. Thus prediction is a major concern of political scientists, especially in cases where it is essential to anticipate the consequences of political actions in order to provide sound advice on policy matters.

Philosophers of science agree that a scientific explanation of an observed event shows that the fact to be explained either follows logically from certain premises or is highly probable based on the premises. Scientific explanations are deductive in structure: they logically connect the premises of an argument with the conclusion. If the premises are true, the conclusion must be true. In addition, science requires that the conclusions implied in a set of premises must be well confirmed by empirical evidence. A sound scientific explanation accounts for an observed fact by showing the fact as one instance of a general tendency. A deductive explanation employs universal laws or generalizations to describe why specific events occur or to predict future occurrences. A statistical or probabilistic explanation shows why the conclusion that follows from certain premises is probable.

Philosophers of science have defined a scientific theory as a set of systematically related statements, including one or more lawlike statements, that are empirically testable. A theory does not replicate reality, but provides a coherent, organized understanding of real events. It consists of axioms and assumptions from which lawlike regularities are derived and then tested against the reality about which one is theorizing. Sound theories contain two features: a structural link between axioms, assumptions, concepts, and derived generalizations, and corroborated empirical content. These attributes can be summarized in philosopher of science Carl Hempel's definition: "Any scientific theory may be conceived as consisting of an uninterpreted, deductively developed system and of an interpretation which confirms empirical import upon the terms and sentences of the latter."[1]

The purpose of scientific theory is to develop empirically useful generalizations. The great power of Newtonian mechanics, for example, resides in a small set of theoretical laws that link mass and motion and thereby explain (by deductive implication) a great number of empirical laws and regularities about bullets, missiles, and planetary motion. Another function of theory is to organize, systematize, and coordinate existing knowledge in a particular area or field. As a theory increases in explanatory power, it becomes part of a system of knowledge. In the process, it suggests new avenues of inquiry by generating hypotheses. A scientific theory thus explains, predicts, organizes, and generates hypotheses for additional inquiry.

Political scientists have developed a large number of different conceptual frameworks, which we have previously listed. While these frameworks are helpful in organizing our thinking about politics and classifying our observations, none is, in the strictest sense, a rigorously developed theory of politics. By no means do we intend to demean these endeavors—all these schools of political analysts have striven for rigor and precision. The closest approximation to a scientific theory of politics can be found, in our judgment, in the rational-choice school, the disciples of which pattern their approach on the assumptions of utility that buttress economic theorizing. The success they have attained to date is relatively limited when compared with the accomplishments of, for example, price theorists. But they began much later and face a more intractable subject—nonmarket decision making. In any event, our purpose is not to criticize our colleagues for their failures to build valid theories of politics, but rather to set forth the objectives and standards of scientific inquiry in order to provide criteria against which we can judge our own work in developing a formal interest group theory of politics and testing it against an important body of evidence. We hope to persuade by example.

POLICY ANALYSIS

Policy analysis is the great growth industry in political science, spurred by the astronomical increase in pubic spending in pursuit of concrete policy objectives during the past two decades. As public spending on social programs in the United States, Western Europe, Japan, and even less developed countries has risen to consume the lion's share of public funds in these nations, politicians, bureaucrats, and scholars alike have tried to ascertain the successes and failures of these programs. Such terms as *the policy agenda*, *implementation*, *evaluation*, *feedback*, and *cost-benefit analysis* have become commonplace.

Current emphasis on policy analysis is a logical culmination of the development of political science. It blends the *is* with the *ought* in taking a specific, socially determined value judgment—in Western democracies, typically reached after majoritarian consideration—about the proper use of public goods and ideas, and then applies scientific know-how in pursuit of those goals. The same holds for dictatorships, save that one man or a ruling committee typically states social objectives with less regard for the wishes of the majority and more ruthlessly pursues those objectives over public opposition.

Public policies are developed by governmental bodies or

officials. They represent purposive or goal-oriented action rather than random or chance behavior. Policy consists of patterns of public action rather than specific decisions, and it also involves decisions about the implementation and enforcement of those patterns. Policy is what governments do, not what they say they are going to do. It may take positive or negative forms—the carrot or the stick. As stated earlier, public policy involves the use of the legally coercive power of government that private organizations do not have.

Public policy analysis encompasses both the various steps that occur in the process of making and enforcing policy and the specific policy outcomes that result. Within this framework, policy formation and implementation involve conflict among individuals and groups with different opinions and desires. Theoretical development in the field of policy analysis not only must help explain the process of making public policy but also must be able to predict the resolution of the conflicts over policy issues.

It is in this spirit that we have written this book. We have tried to develop a formal interest group theory of politics that both explains the process by which policy decisions are made and predicts the specific resolution of the issues that comprise the agenda for collective choice. We have arrayed the theory against the important issue of the future of more than five million Chinese people who live in the British Crown Colony of Hong Kong and who face reabsorption into the Chinese body politic on July 1, 1997, when China reestablishes its sovereign authority. The theory will be tested against several overarching issues and more than a dozen concrete ones that, taken together, will determine Hong Kong's post-1997 economic, political, legal, and social systems. The analysis was completed in March 1984, so we can compare our forecasts with the actual terms of the Sino–British agreement announced in September 1984, some six months later. Using the same analytical tool, we will also attempt to forecast changes within Hong Kong between 1985 and 1997, before China recovers the colony, and after 1997, when Chinese authority will hold full sway.

We believe this book presents a productive way to do political analysis and policy forecasting. Apart from the specific case-study demonstration concerning the future of Hong Kong, we have put together what we hope will become a handbook of policy analysis that others can employ in their own areas of interest. We have made no expert obsolete but have provided a theoretical tool to make more powerful use of that expertise.

2
How to Analyze Politics

In the daily story of politics, interest groups demand and leaders supply decisions. Unlike the marketplace, however, the supply of and demand for policies is often unbalanced. An increase in demand for particular political decisions sometimes makes those decisions more likely, but at other times politicians seem to behave perversely, making choices that run against the press of current demands. Moreover, politicians can and do manipulate the social agenda, creating some demands that did not exist before and quashing others, removing them from discussion despite—or perhaps because of—the apparent strong desire for them. It is no wonder that so many have despaired of creating a predictive science of politics. And yet we propose just such a predictive science here. We will show, with a few inoffensive assumptions, that it is possible to predict political decisions, including specific policy choices and their structural consequences, with subtlety, depth, and accuracy. We will show that it is possible to predict effective and ineffective strategic decisions. It is possible to predict differences in perceptions and the political consequences, both broad and narrow, of those differences. It is possible to show when politicians will underestimate or overestimate their prospects of success (or failure) and the consequences of those estimations for policy formation.

11

APPROACHES TO POLICY FORECASTING

Before turning to the actual analytic approach we propose, it is useful to reflect on how one might go about studying policy formation. What, for instance, are the most desirable characteristics of a tool that aims to predict choices and their consequences?

By far the most important characteristic of any forecasting methodology, whether for predicting the weather or for estimating the likelihood of war, is the accuracy of its predictions. Unfortunately, accuracy is often difficult to measure. Just what do we mean when we ask "was the forecast accurate?" If the weatherman tells us that there is a 50 percent chance of rain, do we take that to mean that it should rain on half the days with such a forecast, or that rain should fall during half of the hours in the day on which the forecast is made? If we predict that the wage rate for Mexico will rise 5 percent from the previous six months, is the forecast accurate if the actual rate goes up 6 percent? What is the appropriate base against which to measure the difference? These are not easy questions to answer. However, we would like to suggest stringent criteria for evaluating the accuracy of forecasts. These criteria, drawn from the research of Imre Lakatos, set down reasonable rules for choosing one approach to a problem over another. The *Lakatos Criteria* are

A scientific theory T is *falsified* if and only if another theory T' has been proposed with the following characteristics: (1) T' has excess empirical content over T: that is, it predicts *novel* facts, that is, facts improbable in the light of, or even forbidden, by T; (2) T' explains the previous success of T, that is, all the unrefuted content of T is included (within the limits of observational error) in the content of T'; and (3) some of the excess content of T' is corroborated.[1]

Using these criteria, it is evident that the quality of prediction is best assessed by comparing the performance of alternative approaches, rather than by holding it up to some absolute standard. The best method is the one that explains the greatest number of phenomena without sacrificing the ability to predict successfully phenomena explained by other methods.

A second desirable characteristic is parsimony, the ability to obtain large amounts of information from few assumptions and data inputs. This quality is desirable because it makes analysis more efficient. The fewer assumptions and the less data needed to obtain new information, the easier it becomes to make successful predictions.

A useful forecasting tool should have considerable power and flexibility. Power is the capability to address with equal ease a wide range of policy questions. It should be possible to employ the same approach in addressing a variety of substantive issues and in dealing with both small and large questions. Ideally, a powerful forecasting tool will handle many different policy settings. Likewise, a forecasting approach should possess the flexibility to ask not only what policy decision will be made, but also how it will be made. A flexible model permits the analyst to simulate various circumstances or background conditions and to evaluate the consequences that follow. For instance, what if a key decision maker alters his or her objectives? Will the subsequent decision change? A flexible tool can handle such "what if" questions with the same facility and accuracy with which it handles actual situations. The expected utility approach adopted here satisfies all of these characteristics. Before turning to the approach, however, it is helpful to examine the methods that policy analysts have previously employed.

The method most frequently used to forecast political decisions is to ask experts what they believe will happen. Such an approach has considerable merit. People who have spent the better part of their professional lives studying a particular problem or region are in command of a vast array of factual information, and their judgments are almost certainly more accurate than the assessments of the average interested layperson. In that sense, expert opinions satisfy the Lakatos Criteria when compared to the "seat-of-the-pants" judgments of less informed individuals. However, the use of experts' judgments is frought with grave risks and limitations.

Experts rarely make explicit the criteria they use to evaluate the information available to them or the criteria they use to select information in the first place. Different experts often provide different information for a specific forecast or policy analysis. Because the assumptions and the analytic structure are essentially invisible, there is no meaningful way for the forecaster to choose among differing analyses. And even when the same expert repeats his or her research, he or she may not bring the same perspective to the problem the next time. Thus, scholars cannot build a systematic body of knowledge and expectations from expert analysis. Judgments differ from individual to individual and from time to time.

Largely in response to the many recognized shortcomings of the "expert approach," policy analysts have turned recently to statistical or econometric techniques for assessing policy decisions. These approaches force scholars to make explicit assumptions about the structure of the information needed to evaluate any given policy problem, and thus they resolve one of the major shortcomings of the expert approach. However, the solution is not wholly satisfactory. While statistical methods insure that data-related assumptions are explicit, the thought processes that govern the analysis still remain invisible. Beyond plausible, but chiefly casual, arguments, statistical approaches to forecasting rarely make explicit the precise logic governing the selection of variables or of ways to combine them. Moreover, because such approaches to policy analysis almost invariably assume that a curve can be fit through some data and then extrapolated into the future, statistical forecasting proves rather accurate for stable trends, but generally proves unreliable in forecasting significant shifts in policy. But the shifts are often of the greatest interest. A better method would be equally capable of predicting stable "no change" situations, stable "incremental change" situations, and unstable, "sharp change" situations. A forecasting approach capable of accurate prediction in all of those situations would satisfy the Lakatos criteria by corroborating the results of expert or statistical methods, while adding considerable additional content.

To achieve the goals of the Lakatos Criteria, a method must be developed that is explicit about the logic governing the selection of variables, the way they are combined, and how the analytic results are interpreted. An expected utility model of policy analysis meets these objectives. It contains an explicit, axiomatic structure that has been well developed in microeconomics. The approach permits scholars to deduce both intuitive and counterintuitive results concerning policy formation, and allows them to observe and empirically evaluate the results with only modest amounts of data. Because the logic of the approach is fully specified at every step in the process of constructing a policy forecast, our mathematical—but not statistical—modeling method allows us to study the effect of each element in the analysis on the overall policy evaluation. Nothing is hidden, either from the analyst or from those who are interested in the results. The method also dictates the selection of information, which experts may provide.

Experts are indispensable for the expected utility approach to political analysis. Even when consensus exists on the essential facts, experts often disagree about the conclusions they draw. The expected utility approach only relies on their knowledge of the facts. The approach provides a coherent justification and explanation for the interpretation of results regardless of the level of agreement among experts. At the same time, a deductive, axiomatic, mathematical modeling approach enjoys all the strengths of statistical or econometric modeling, without the limitations of largely ad hoc arguments driving any particular statistical technique. In sum, the expected utility approach fosters accurate, detailed, parsimonious, flexible political analysis and policy forecasting in both theory and practice.

ASSUMPTIONS

Building a method for political analysis requires some assumptions about how politics is structured. Some of these assumptions are not fully satisfied in the real world all of the time. Of course, it is not the purpose of assumptions to replicate reality, but rather to impose a simplifying structure that grasps the *essential* elements of reality. The frailty or robustness of these assumptions is an empirical matter, not a theoretical one. Assumptions that provide useful insights into reality and generate accurate predictions are justified.

We assume:

1. Competition between groups produces political decisions.
2. Groups compete over specific policy-related issues.
3. A strong leader dominates each group.
4. Each strong leader is a rational decision maker who seeks to maximize expected utility.

The first assumption draws out an important difference between economics and politics. Recall from chapter 1 that exchanges in a marketplace require cooperation between buyers and sellers. A deal is consummated only when it satisfies all parties to the exchange. In the absence of a monopoly or governmental restraint, buyers are free to choose among competing vendors and competing baskets of goods. The buyer is driven by his or her desires and constrained by his or her pocketbook. Likewise, the seller is free to reject a buyer who does not offer an acceptable price for his or her goods. In politics, however, coercion and power are the currencies of accomplishment. Decision makers can force others to "consume" policy "goods" they do not want. Politics is inherently a game of competition and coercion. Of course, cooperation also plays a role in policy formation. Groups with similar interests frequently coalesce to defeat what they view as obnoxious alternatives. But if a choice must be made from among these groups' preferred alternatives, coalitions break apart, sundered by their competing interests just as surely as those interests—when pitted against still other options—joined them together. In politics, yesterday's enemies are frequently today's friends, only to become tomorrow's enemies. It is in this sense that politics is competitive and noncooperative. Cooperation, when it exists, is merely an expedient to a later phase of competition among the erstwhile collaborators.

Political activity is competition between groups over policy-related issues. It is not merely a quest for personal victory. Policy positions are more than mere instruments for achieving power or control over the perquisites of office. Without power, it is difficult to attain specific policy objectives. However, pursuit of power in its own right is often self-defeating. We assume that politicians try to create a maximally useful mix of their ambition for power and their ambition to institute or enforce certain policies. It may well be that those most concerned about policy, rather than power, risk losing power as the result of openly stating their objectives on specific issues. For example, candidates often get in trouble when they advocate concrete solutions to such contentious issues as abortion, defense spending, prayer in the schools, and so forth. In making this assumption, we do not, of course, imply any normative judgment about the relative merits of seeking power at the expense of policy goals or of standing for particular policy choices at the expense of almost certain defeat. Indeed, while we believe that, in the long run, successful policies are likely to lead to power, we also believe that politicans generally have a short time horizon, which inclines them to trade off between their policy goals and their political ambitions.

In an issue-oriented view of politics, groups are defined as amalgamations of individuals pursuing some common policy objectives. Thus, a group is any entity, from one individual to many millions, that shares a common array of priorities on one or more issues. In the parlance of social choice theorists, a group is a set of individuals with a common preference ordering over relevant issues. Shortly we will elaborate other characteristics of a group, but for now we will focus on this one.

Because we assume all members of a group have the same preferences concerning certain policy issues, each group thus speaks with one voice on those issues. The group's unanimity implies that the desires of any one member concerning those issues constitutes an accurate representation of the whole body. Therefore, for the sake of simplicity, we assume each group is headed by a strong leader whose personal policy objectives are synonymous with those of the group as a whole. Bureaucratic infighting is a daily occurrence in politics, but its presence does not vitiate this assumption. Quite the contrary, the strong leader assumption illuminates the logical properties of bureaucratic politics. Thus, if an organization consists of several factions, we treat each faction as if it were a separate group. The strong leader assumption represents each bureaucratic interest as a separate, competing entity with its own group preferences and resources which it brings to bear on policy formation. Therefore, any entity that constitutes a group must satisfy three criteria:

1. On the issue in question, the group's members must agree on the order in which alternatives are preferred.
2. A group must control some pool of relevant political, economic, and/or military resources which it can employ in pursuit of its objectives.
3. A group must comprise a set of individuals (from one to any number) who agree on how much effort to expend in order to achieve their objectives.

A group must satisfy all three of these conditions. Factions exist if there is disagreement over goals, or over what resources should be spent to achieve common goals, or if significantly different resource pools can be mobilized by different individuals or sub-groups within the body.

The final assumption is that each leader is rational. Rationality posits that each person rates alternatives as more or less desirable and chooses his or her most preferred alternative. Obviously, a first choice is preferred to a second, and a second to a third in any list of alternatives, and, by inference, the first is preferred to the third. Social choice theorists describe rational decision makers as holding connected, transitive preferences. Rational decision makers not only select their most preferred alternative, they also act on their preferences to accomplish what they *believe* is in their best interest. We emphasize *believe* to point out that in our model, as in the real world, rational decision makers are perfectly capable of making decisions that, in retrospect, seem wrong or even foolish. We do not assume that leaders who try to make or influence policy choices have special knowledge or insight. Nor do we assume that two leaders, each with the same information and even identical preferences, must necessarily make the same decision. Rationality does not require uniformity of behavior, but it requires that decision makers calculate the costs and benefits of the alternatives open to them and choose the one that seems to yield the greatest advantage.

THE EXPECTED UTILITY DECISION MODEL

The expected utility model proposed here is sufficiently general to forecast the results of almost any policy question at any level of politics. Examples include such areas of economic concern as minimum wage laws or price stability, as well as more directly political concerns, for example, intergovernmental agreements to share technology or to extend military basing rights to other governments. The scope of issues may affect a single nation, a small group (cabinet, union, or boardroom), or international relations.

For each policy, the expected utility approach requires basic information on

1. identification of the relevant internal or external political actors who may wish to influence this policy.
2. a specified range of policy alternatives that encompasses all possible outcomes (i.e., that encompasses the most extreme positions taken by any of the groups).
3. the policy preference of each group on the issue.
4. estimates of the relative political, economic, or military capabilities that each group may employ to influence the policy decision.
5. estimates of the importance (salience) each group attaches to each issue, signifying the group's interest in influencing policy outcomes.

This list is neither surprising nor esoteric. Most policy analysts use these fundamental elements in their work, whether or not they employ a structured model into which they can plug these data. These elements contain information about which experts tend to agree, even when they disagree over likely policy outcomes. But, while the identification of groups' positions and resources is valuable in and of itself, such information is more valuable still when it is incorporated into a comprehensive theory of politics. What would a rigorous method of analyzing politics accomplish? It would

1. analyze what policy choices are most likely to be made and implemented.

2. examine the process (whether orderly or violent) by which policy choices are reached.
3. identify what political realignments may result from a forecasted policy decision and what the implications of these new alignments might be.
4. evaluate the significance of alternative data inputs or assumptions in order to assess the degree of confidence associated with the policy forecasts derived.

The expected utility model that follows addresses all of these issues. The theoretical framework for the decision model, based on the tenets of microeconomic theory, assumes that decision makers strive to obtain the largest net gain based upon an evaluation of the costs and benefits associated with choices, taking into account what is for them an acceptable level of risk. This framework assesses each group's perception of the likely actions of all other groups. It defines the environment in which policy choices are made. The model structures estimates of the policymaker's anticipated gains or losses from challenging policy positions preferred by other groups. This expected utility calculation for each group relevant to a particular issue may be partially represented with the decision model depicted in figure 2.1.

The figure depicts a group leader's calculations of the costs and benefits associated with challenging some other group's policy position—for example, the position of the government. The figure represents a debate as being limited to discussions between "the challenger" and "the government." In a strictly two-way exchange, the challenging group weighs the probability that it will succeed in moving the government to accept the challenger's policy preference and assesses how much value it derives from getting the government to change its policy. Naturally, the greater the separation between the challenger and the government, the more value the challenger gets from convincing the government to alter its policy stance. At the same time, the challenger also weighs the probability that it will fail to bring about a change in the government's policy. By failing, the challenger may be compelled to move its own position closer to that of the government leadership. The costs of defeat are directly

Figure 2.1

The Decision Problem

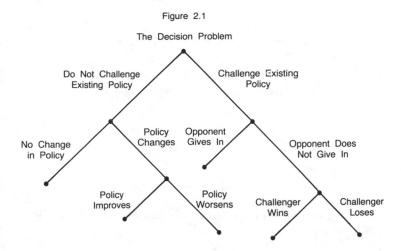

related to the gap in position separating the two parties to the exchange.

These calculations, in turn, are pitted against the likely consequences if the challenger does nothing. In the event of inaction, the government's policy may remain unchanged. It is also possible that the government will alter its position in response to pressures or preferences stemming from other groups. Should the challenger anticipate such a change in governmental policy, it must assess the value and the likelihood of the government's moving closer to or further from the challenger's goals. The sequence underlying these calculations is represented in figure 2.1. However, this figure does not take into account the potential impact of other groups on the challenger's behavior.

Figure 2.2 depicts the calculations necessary to estimate the *marginal impact of third parties* on the challenger's welfare in the event the option to do nothing is rejected. The challenger must estimate the impact of each third party under the assumptions that third parties aid either the government or the challenger. The difference between the two assumptions represents the net marginal impact of each third party.

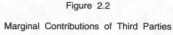

Figure 2.2

Marginal Contributions of Third Parties

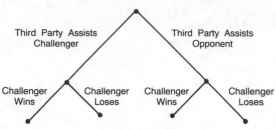

The calculations depicted in the two decision trees can be summarized verbally as follows:

Expected Net Gain =
(Probability of success) × (Possible policy gains)
+ (Probability of failure) × (Possible policy setbacks)
+ (Net expected marginal impact of third parties)
− {(Probability of policy remaining unchanged if this group does nothing) × (Value of current policy)
+ (Probability of policy changing if this group does nothing) × [(Probability of policy improving if this group does nothing) × (Value of anticipated improvement)
+ (Probability of policy worsening if this group does nothing) × (Value of anticipated deterioration)]}

This verbal statement can be expressed mathematically. Letting P_s denote the probability of success, and U_s and U_f respectively denote the value, or utility, of success and failure, we may represent the generic expected utility from challenging existing policy as:

$$E(U)_c = P_s(U_s) + (1 - P_s)(U_f)$$

An equivalent calculation exists for the strategy of not challenging existing policy. Let P_q be the anticipated probability that current policy will not change; let U_q denote the utility associated with the continuation of existing policy; let P_b be the likelihood that policy is expected to change for the better, with the value of the anticipated improvement being U_b and the value of any anticipated worsening of current policy being U_w. Then, the expected utility from not challenging current policy is:

$$E(U)_{nc} = P_q(U_q) + (1 - P_q)[P_b(U_b) + (1 - P_b)(U_w)]$$

Denoting that calculation as $E(U)_{nc}$, the overall expected utility calculation may be summarized as:

$$E(U) = E(U)_c - E(U)_{nc}$$

As this simplified structure demonstrates, it is rational to undertake a challenge when the expected gains from a challenge exceed the expected value of inaction. The detailed mathematics underlying these generic equations can be found in Appendix A at the end of this chapter.

The verbal equation outlined above is, in reality, one of four very similar equations required to solve our model. The full model encompasses the following four forms:

1. *The Challenger's Welfare* equation estimates what the challenger believes it can extract from (or give to) its opponent.
2. *The Challenger's View of the Opponent's Welfare* equation estimates what the challenger believes its opponent expects to extract from (or give to) the challenger.
3. *The Opponent's Welfare* equation estimates what the opponent believes it can extract from (or give to) the challenger.
4. *The Opponent's View of the Challenger's Welfare* equation estimates what the opponent perceives the challenger expects to extract from (or give to) the opponent.

Because equations 1 and 2 approximate the challenger's view of the situation, and 3 and 4 estimate how the opponent sees things, scenarios can be constructed that take into account differences in perceptions.

FORECASTING THE PROCESS OF POLICY CHANGE

Taken together, the four equations provide estimates of the likely resolution of almost any issue, including the specific decisions that will be made and how the resolution will affect the policy environment. This section analyzes the impact of policy decisions on the political environment. The next section discusses how to construct policy forecasts.

Consider how a given configuration of expected utility calculations might bring about a change in policy. Will, for instance, the change be strongly contested, or will the transition to a new policy be smooth? This question links two important components: the degree of confidence that the existing policy will continue, and how much each group favoring a change expects to gain or lose. The combination of these two elements provide important information on (a) the intensity of the struggle over a policy shift; (b) the likelihood that the policy will change; and (c) the nature and extent of any compromise that results. Figure 2.3 presents the dynamics of this process in schematic form. Although drawn from the perspective of the government (and so based on equations 3 and 4), it could also be drawn from the perspective of any actor.

In figure 2.3, the values plotted along the horizontal axis represent the net gain or loss expected by the government (or any opponent) in pursuing policy objectives that other groups may resist. The values plotted along the vertical axis represent the government's perception of challengers' expected gains or losses from fighting government policy. Thus any point plotted in the space defined by these axes represents what the government believes it stands to gain or lose vis-á-vis a given challenger, and what the government believes the challenger expects to gain or lose on the issue in question. Values (points) to the right of the vertical axis signify that the government expects to improve its net utility position in pursuit of its objective; it believes that prospective gains exceed potential losses from a challenge. Likewise, values above the horizontal axis imply that the government anticipates that the opponent expects to realize more gains than losses from challenging the government. Values to the left of the vertical axis entail larger losses than gains for the government, and values below the horizontal axis similarly affect the government's perception of the challenger's welfare.

The values plotted in the Cartesian graph of the figure are determined by the solution to equations 3 and 4. Later we

Figure 2.3

Political Dynamics of the Policy Process

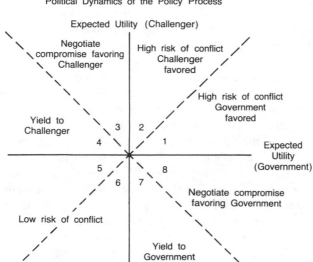

explain how each of the components in those equations is estimated; for now the important point is that the values being
plotted are the mathematical results of solving the relevant
equations. Having plotted the point that represents the relationship between the government's expectations for itself and the
government's estimate of the expectations of each potential
challenger, the likelihood of conflict or instability as a function of
the location and distribution of points can be specified. This can
be done regardless of the content of the issue or the institutional
arrangements and cultural foundations of the society. This makes
possible genuine comparative politics.

Of course, culture, history, institutions, and issues are important. These factors structure the particular orientations of the
interest groups that ultimately determine political behavior. Each
of these elements is "captured" in the mathematical structure of
our approach. For example, the equations show that some societies have highly contentious politics in which key groups take

extreme stands. To say that politics is contentious means, in the model, that some groups are willing to take high risks to attain their objectives. In technical parlance, the society's political culture is tilted toward risk-acceptant behavior. Societies with more cautious political cultures are characterized by a preponderance of risk-averse leaders.

How do institutions affect willingness to accept risk? Plurality voting systems encourage leaders and candidates to adopt cautious, centrist policies because those taking extreme positions are invariably defeated by more moderate elements. For example, the public's perceptions that 1964 presidential candidate Barry Goldwater might be willing to use nuclear weapons in Southeast Asia, and that George McGovern would follow an appeasement policy in Southeast Asia in 1972, contributed to these candidates' overwhelming losses. In plurality democratic systems, winners must attract the bulk of the votes from those located in the middle of the political spectrum. By contrast, democratic systems with proportional representation encourage more extreme, risk-acceptant behavior. In such systems, extremist candidates can gain office in proportion to their share of the overall vote, although in a plurality system they are sure to lose. A plurality system yields but one winner per contest, no matter how close the results, whereas proportional representation can yield many winners. Likewise, some authoritarian arrangements foster moderate behavior, while others foster extremism. These distinctions are represented in our model by the structure of the utility and probability terms. They are not represented by ad hoc, "tacked on" variables.

Despite the apparent "sterility" of our mathematical approach, it has generated accurate, detailed, often subtle predictions in hundreds of real-world cases; that is, it truly forecasts the future. The model is equally at home in explaining past events. It has been applied to a wide variety of international conflicts with considerable success. It has yielded counterintuitive propositions that were subsequently borne out and that became widely accepted as explanations of past behavior.[2] Most scholars believe that it is easier to explain the past than predict the future. Therefore, the model's success in forecasting a wide variety of future events gives us confidence in its value as a tool for analyzing politics.

One test of the model's effectiveness involved predicting the size of the budget deficit to be approved by the Italian Parliament and its subsequent effect on the stability of the sitting government. In September 1982 the model forecast a sequence of events that led to the fall of the Spadolini government on the deficit issue. It predicted that Spadolini would give way to a government led by Fanfani, who would approve a 70-trillion-lira deficit, and that Fanfani's coalition would dissolve as the Communist party shifted its economic policies rightward. In late fall, 1982, Spadolini's government fell, and, to the surprise of most Italian experts, who had forecast a Socialist government led by Craxi, it was replaced by a Christian Democratic government led by Fanfani. In early 1983, as predicted, the Italian Parliament passed a budget with a deficit of 70.5 trillion lira, when responsible debate encompassed a range from 60 to 80 trillion lira. Finally, Fanfani fell, as predicted, due to a Communist shift to the right. It is important to stress that the events of early 1983 were fully anticipated in September 1982.[3]

A second illustration concerned the response of the Mexican government to an austerity program that the International Monetary Fund demanded as its price for assisting Mexico, which was burdened with enormous external debt due to its foreign exchange crisis. The model accurately predicted that President De La Madrid's government would drastically reduce real wages, hold food and fuel subsidies substantially below the inflation rate (thus raising their real costs), and crack down on corruption. Forecasts were performed on a quarterly basis beginning in the waning months of President Portillo's regime, and results were published months before any other commentator described the unfolding of De La Madrid's political strength in the course of his implementation of the severe austerity and corruption crackdown programs. The press reported these events with great surprise! The forecasts not only anticipated the change in government policies, they also described the specific changes that De La Madrid would accept due to pressures from particular elements within his coalition.[4]

The model also predicted the shifts in strategy to economic warfare in the Iran/Iraq War;[5] the uprising by supporters of Ayatollah Shariatmadari in Tabriz against the regime of Ayatollah Khomeini in December 1979;[6] and the choice of Yuri Andropov to succeed Leonid Brezhnev as the Soviet leader.[7]

In short, the model has successfully predicted several important political events, with an overall success rate exceeding 90 percent. It has successfully predicted outcomes in a wide variety of cultural, institutional, and other environmental settings. It is, in short, a way to analyze politics. The approach is equally successful whether applied to rich or poor countries, to democratic or authoritarian states, to capitalist or socialist economies, to Western, "materialist" societies or to sectarian theocracies. It marries the institutional and historical expertise of country specialists with the mathematical rigor of axiomatic theorizing so that the strengths of each complement rather than compete with the other.

INTERPRETING THE EXPECTED UTILITY GRAPHS

The following pages graphically display the political dynamics that are embodied within the four expected utility equations. The four equations explain the political factors of give and take that culminate in a policy decision. The graphs show when issues are contentious or easily resolved. For the expected utility values plotted in each of the eight octants depicted in figure 2.3, we may interpret the results as follows.

Octants 1 and 2. The actor on the horizontal axis, the government in this example, believes that it stands to benefit in a contest against a would-be challenger. However, the government also believes that the opponent expects to succeed in contesting the regime. Situations falling in octant 1 favor the government; those in octant 2 the challenger. Cases falling within this portion of the graph face a high risk of conflict. After all, if each side thinks it will be the winner in a policy disagreement, neither side has an incentive to give in to the other. Nor has either side much incentive to reduce its demands and accept a compromise settlement. In an international context, disputes that fall within this region of the graph have escalated into war about 90 percent of the time.[8]

Figure 2.4 illustrates this potential for conflict in the Italian budget-deficit example previously discussed.[9] Note that all government–challenger interactions fall within octants 1 and 2. In early fall, 1982, Prime Minister Spadolini believed that every potential challenger in Italy expected to defeat his government on critical budget-deficit legislation. Spadolini, however, thought he could defeat all potential opponents. In November, Spadolini's government fell on a vote of no confidence, bringing about a political crisis that was resolved by the formation of a Christian Democratic government, which was defeated in turn by a coalition of Socialist and Communist Party forces in the spring of 1983.

Octants 5 and 6. In contrast to octants 1 and 2, situations in octants 5 and 6 reveal that both the challenger and the government expect to lose in a dispute with one another. Consequently, each side has an incentive to posture or float trial balloons, but not to attempt real action. Policy discussions that meet these conditions are very unlikely to escalate into serious disputes and pose virtually no threat to the stability of the government.

Figure 2.5 illustrates a forecast of the future of the Marcos regime in the Philippines, looking at the issue from the perspective of his opponents. (These perspectives are derived from equations 1 and 2.) This analysis, done several months before the spring 1984 elections in the Philippines, indicates that most of the opposition did not believe it could defeat Marcos.[10] Indeed, efforts to boycott the elections proved unsuccessful, while the elections themselves stimulated considerably less violence and disruption than most analysts expected.

Octant 3. The actor on the horizontal axis, the government in figure 2.6, believes that it faces defeat by the challenger. The government also believes that the challenger concurs in this view. However, the government feels that its concessions on policy need not be as great as the opposition seems to require. Examine figure 2.6. Line *AX* represents the value the government attaches to the gains seemingly demanded by some opponent, while line *BY* represents the value the government

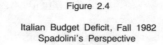

Figure 2.4

Italian Budget Deficit, Fall 1982
Spadolini's Perspective

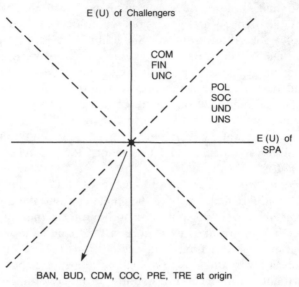

BAN, BUD, CDM, COC, PRE, TRE at origin

Groups:		POL	Political press
		PRE	Pertini
BAN	Bank of Italy	SOC	Socialists
BUD	Ministry of Budget	SPA	Spadolini
COC	Employer's Association	TRE	Treasury Ministry
COM	Communists	UNC	Communist unions
CDM	Christian Democrats	UND	Christian Democrat unions
FIN	Financial press	UNS	Socialist unions

attaches to its own expected losses. Point AB is the intersection
of the two expectations. Line segment PQ represents an equilib-
rium in which gains and losses are precisely equal. The government is prepared to give up just enough on the policy under
dispute so that it suffers a utility loss exactly equal to B. It must
also be prepared to tolerate a utility transfer to its opponent that
equals its own loss. Denoting that transfer as B', the actual
dispute (as seen by the government) between the government

Figure 2.5

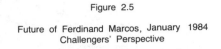

Future of Ferdinand Marcos, January 1984
Challengers' Perspective

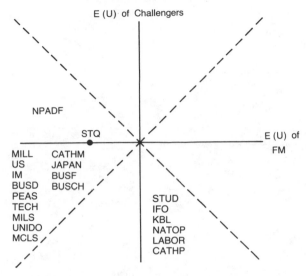

Groups:

		MCLS	Middle class
		MILL	Loyal military
BUSCH	Chinese business community	MILS	Skeptical military elements
BUSD	Philippine business community	NATOP	Nationalist Opposition
BUSF	Foreign business community	NPADF	New People's Army / National
CATHM	Catholic moderates		Democratic Front
CATHP	Catholic progressives	PEAS	Peasants
FM	Ferdinand Marcos	STQ	Status quo
IFO	World Bank and IMF	STUD	Students
IM	Imelda Romualdez Marcos	TECH	Technocrats
JAPAN	Japan	UNIDO	United Nationalist Democratic
KBL	New Society movement		Opposition
LABOR	Urban labor	US	United States

and the challenger is over the difference between *A* and *B'*. The specific settlement will therefore fall somewhere in the outlined space *AB'CD*. Such situations do not encourage capitulation by the government, but they provide incentives for a negotiated compromise. Such a compromise nevertheless represents a substantial policy defeat for the government.

Figure 2.6

Political Dynamics of Policy Concessions in Octants 3 and 4

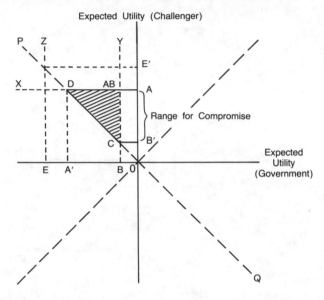

Octant 4. These situations rarely occur when the government is the object of focus. Situations fall in octant 4 when the actor on the horizontal axis, the government in this illustration, believes it could lose even more on the issue in question than the challenger apparently demands. Return to figure 2.6. The challenger's gains are seen to fall on line AX, indicating to the government that the challenger's appetite for concessions can be satisfied if the government transfers A' to the opponent ($OA = A'O$). The government believes its own losses lie on line EZ; therefore it expects the opponent to demand as much as E'. Rather than fight, in which case it expects to lose E, it readily concedes A', which it believes satisfies the challenger's initial demand. In other words, the government gives in, conceding A' of its utility (which it views as transferring A utiles to the challenger) to avoid the greater loss of E, which the government believes it can be made to suffer. To repeat, so long as the

government believes that the challenger can force even larger policy concessions, the government has a very strong incentive to capitulate to the demands of the opposition. These situations do not produce violence or forceful resignations, but they frequently provoke instability. Governments that face octant 4 situations vis-á-vis their opponents rarely survive. They peacefully relinquish control over the institutions of government rather than risk the even larger defeats that they believe the opposition is capable of inflicting on them.

Octant 7. When octant 7 conditions occur, the government believes it is making reasonable demands of its opponents and expects them to capitulate. (It should be evident that situations in octant 7 are analogous to those in octant 4, except that in the latter the advantage resides in the hands of the opposition. The same holds for octants 8 and 3.) From the perspective of the government, the opposition thinks it could be forced to lose even more than the government requests. Such situations, when correctly perceived, are almost always stable. They are quite common, reflecting the strength and commanding position that governments frequently hold. Figure 2.5, for example, shows that many opposition groups reluctantly saw themselves having to accept Marcos's view of the future of Philippine government. It is likely that the absence of widespread violence during the 1984 elections in the Philippines reflected the degree to which students, labor, and the other anti-Marcos factions in octant 7 believed their situation was hopeless at that time.

Octant 8. In cases that fall in octant 8, as in octant 7, the opposition apparently accepts the inevitability of domination by the government, although the situation differs from octant 7 in that the opposition does not believe it must simply yield to the government. Instead, the opposition seems prepared to give up less than the government expects to gain. The two sides agree on who will win but disagree on how much will be won. This circumstance is amenable to a negotiated compromise. However, if the negotiations fail to close the gap between the expectations of the government and the degree of loss acceptable to thc opposition, instability which tends to reinforce the government's advantage may follow.

Knowing how groups fall into the eight Cartesian spaces permits both description and explanation of the circumstances that surround each policy decision. Keep in mind that assignment of groups to one of the eight octants is fully determined by the equations. The mathematical relations among the expected utility values determine the construction of the Cartesian coordinate system itself as well as the configuration of each octant. The interpretation of each octant, in turn, follows directly from the logic of the model, not from intuition or statistical criteria of goodness of fit. The model transcends issues, institutions, and unique historical and sociological factors in the society in question. It has been successfully applied to such disparate societies as Italy, the Philippines, and Mexico. It has illuminated both routine policy questions and extraordinary issues capable of bringing down governments.

FORECASTING POLICY OUTCOMES

Recall that the model requires data about the position and power of each group on individual issues. Assume that each group's ambition is to see the policy outcome shift to its preferred position. The potential for the group to gain from a shift depends on the difference between the importance it attaches to its preferred outcome (defined to equal 1.0) and the degree of preference it attaches to each possible alternative result. The value attached to each possible outcome is calculated by correlating each challenger's ranking of alternatives with the rankings of each other group's preferences. This procedure assumes that a group's preference for alternative outcomes steadily rises as those outcomes approach its most preferred position. Thus, the closer the preferred positions of two groups and the more similar their ordering of alternatives, the more value they are assumed to attach to each other's success. One way to quantify this similarity of interests is the standard Pearson product-moment correlation coefficient.

The numerical quantity just described becomes the first critical building block in our estimation of a full utility function. Later we develop the second building block—the extent to which decision makers are willing to accept risks. The correlation representing the degree of similarity of goals is a fundamental element in the development of our policy forecasts. This correlation represents the utility for an outcome in the absence of risk.

Treat the policy-formation process as if it were a voting procedure. Assume each group has assessed the acceptability of alternatives. This assessment is made after the political maneuvering depicted in the Cartesian coordinate graphs has taken place. We assume that these political struggles clarify what groups can truly accomplish, thereby eliminating differences in perception that result from different orientations toward risk-taking. Thus, the correlation coefficients represent the final evaluation of alternatives after each group learns, through political struggles, what it is capable of accomplishing.

Now think of the selection of a policy as an exercise in voting. Whereas each member of a legislature has one and only one vote, in the expected utility model, voters (groups) are endowed with variable numbers of votes. Moreover, voters are not restricted to voting fully for or fully against an alternative— they may also cast partial votes. We assume that the "number of votes" (i.e., the power) possessed by each group depends on the relevant capability it can bring to bear on the issue. Thus, an issue under contest in a political arena faces a vote based partially on the distribution of political influence. This notion of voting is not necessarily a vote in the liberal, democratic sense of the word. While such voting is encompassed by our meaning, we have in mind simply that groups mobilize and use some of their resources to influence decisions, depending upon the extent to which they prefer one alternative over another.

The importance of an issue to a group will, not surprisingly, affect how much of its capabilities it is willing to spend. Thus, the higher the issue's *salience*, the more a group will invest. Indifference between alternatives will produce abstention—groups will not waste votes (resources). The weaker (stronger) its preference for any alternative over another, the fewer (more) votes it will cast.

How might such a policy "vote" look in our framework? To answer this question, examine a hypothetical issue concerning internal Chinese politics. The hypothetical data presented here represent attitudes on China's modernization program versus maintenance of its ideological purity. Figures 2.7 and 2.8 depict the hypothetically preferred position of each critical group within China, as well as the importance each attaches to the issue. In this example, Deng Xiaoping's second choice (after his own hypothetical modernization goal) is the position taken by the army, which is closest to his own. Deng's next-preferred alternative is the position of the Guangdong provincial leadership (GPL). He least supports the hypothetical position of the Communist party ideologues.

Table 2.1 transforms the information portrayed spatially in figure 2.7 into estimates of the "utility" each group attaches to the positions taken by other groups (denoted by U_j^i). We place the word *utility* in quotation marks to remind the reader that at

Figure 2.7
Hypothetical Issue: Position Continuum

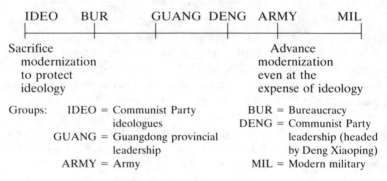

Groups: IDEO = Communist Party   BUR = Bureaucracy
                        ideologues   DENG = Communist Party
               GUANG = Guangdong provincial   leadership (headed
                          leadership   by Deng Xiaoping)
              ARMY = Army   MIL = Modern military

Figure 2.8
Hypothetical Issue: Salience Continuum

Table 2.1.   Hypothetical Issue: Preliminary "Utility"
and Group Power Scores

Preliminary "Utility" Scores*					
	IDEO	BUR	GUANG	DENG	ARMY	MIL
IDEO	—	.94	.09	−.60	−.66	−1.00
BUR	.94	—	.14	−.54	−.60	−.94
GUANG	.09	.14	—	.66	.60	−.09
DENG	−.60	−.54	.66	—	.94	.60
ARMY	−.66	−.60	.60	.94	—	.66
MIL	−1.00	−.94	−.09	.60	.66	—

Group Power Estimates					
	IDEO	BUR	GUANG	DENG	ARMY	MIL
Power	6	28	4	43	9	11

*Read utility scores for each group by beginning in the row and reading across to
the appropriate column. The number represents the row group's "utility" for the
alternative supported by the column group. Although the row/column and
column/row "utility" scores are symmetric in this illustration, utility scores are
not usually symmetric in actual analyses. Group power estimates do not add up to
100 due to rounding error.

this juncture the concept is based only on the correlation of
preferences across the alternatives. When the risk-taking component is added, giving us a full utility function, we will use the term
without quotation marks around it.

Figure 2.8 shows that Deng attaches much less importance
to this issue than does the bureaucracy, which attaches more
importance to it than does either faction of the military. This
information is used to weight the amount of resources each group
will spend to resolve the issue. Finally, note each group's power
score, depicted in table 2.1. This score represents expert judgments about the relative influence of each group. Thus, if one
group scores 50 and another scores 25, the first is twice as
influential as the second.

In the case of an internal political debate between the GPL
and the army over this hypothetical policy issue, Deng would
throw his weight behind the army, because their position is closer
to his than is that of the GPL. But how strongly will Deng's
preference influence the outcome? Perhaps his desires will be

decisive. After all, China is not a democracy and Deng seems to be the most powerful person in China today. That, however, would not be our answer. Deng's power derives, in part, from his ability to pick and choose the issues on which he will take a strong stand. In this case, our approach suggests that Deng will favor the army, but not by much. Table 2.1 shows that his "utility" (i.e., his preference) for the army over the GPL is very slight. In fact, subtracting the two quantities (.94 − .66) shows his preference is only .28. Weighting this similarity of objectives (the correlation coefficient) by his relative power (43) and by the importance he attaches to the issue (.10) leads to the conclusion that Deng would cast 43 × .10 × .28 votes for a total of about 1.20 votes in favor of the army.

Intuitively, groups are likely to attach varying degrees of salience to different issues—groups do not equally care about every possible issue. But the logical structure of the model presented in this book does not constrain groups from asserting that they attach maximum salience to every issue. Despite this limitation, the forecasts turn out to be quite accurate. Hence, it is reasonable to assume that groups express their true salience on issues, rather than bluffing by acting as if they care more than they do. Future versions of the model will incorporate this constraint rather than treating it as an assumption. For now, however, we assume that when a group goes for broke by committing lots of resources and loses, it risks weakness on future votes because it has fewer resources left to invest. Moreover, to the victor goes the spoils. Winners may be able to take resources away from losers, thus altering the distribution of power.

Each group similarly calculates how many votes to spend on this issue. The Communist Party ideologues, for instance, control only 6 percent of the available political power in the Chinese system, but they attach considerable importance to the issue (.97 from Figure 2.8) and their intensity of preference is rather large. They strongly dislike the army's position ("utility" of −.66), and modestly like the position of the GPL. Their total commitment in a dispute over these two alternatives leads them to make a much greater effort than Deng, whose salience on this dispute is low, is hypothesized to make. Thus, the intensity of preference is

(−.66) − .09 = −.75. (The negative sign in the result indicates that the second of the two alternatives is more preferred, meaning that the ideologues will throw their weight behind the Guangdong provincial leadership in this hypothetical contest.) Their total vote equals 6 × .97 × (−.75), or more than 4 votes in favor of the position taken by the GPL. In this contest, then, the relatively weak Communist Party ideologues actually can exert greater influence than the relatively powerful Deng Xiaoping and his supporters within the Party leadership.

Repeating this calculation for each group reveals whether the GPL's position or the army's position has more total support. Table 2.2 shows this calculation across each group that must choose how to behave in a contest between the policy objective of the GPL and that of the army. These calculations demonstrate that the army's preference will be soundly defeated in this contest. Indeed, the GPL's objective is able to defeat the preferred position of each other group in head-to-head contests. By changing positions on an issue, a form of "sophisticated" voting, groups may enhance their prospects for success. A powerful element of this model is that it allows one to simulate alternative strategies and their consequences. Using such simulation, another group might be able to overcome the GPL's initial advantage through such strategic behavior as temporarily changing its position.

Performing the above calculations across all potentially competing positions reveals the policy stance most likely to succeed.

Table 2.2.   Votes for a Hypothetical Dispute

Group	Power *	Salience *	Difference in Utility =	Votes*
IDEO	6	.97	−0.75	−4.37
BUR	28	.97	−0.74	−20.10
GUANG	4	.50	−0.40	−0.80
DENG	43	.10	0.28	1.20
ARMY	9	.15	0.40	0.54
MIL	11	.15	0.75	1.24
Total Votes				−22.29

*Negative numbers signify a preference for the position of the GPL over that of the army. Positive numbers signify the opposite.

That position is the model's forecast of the policy decision. Now we present a more precise description of the process by which a forecast is derived.

Let U^i_j = the "utility" (the correlation measuring the similarity of preferences) of group i for the array of alternatives pursued by group j. Each group, in turn, is represented by i, with each other group becoming j. Possible values range between -1 and $+1$.

Let S_i = the salience, or importance, that i attaches to the issue in question. Possible values range between 0 and 1, representing the probability that i will spend its resources on the issue in question.

Let Cap^i = the proportion of relevant resources controlled by i. Then

$$V^i = (Cap^i) \times S_i \times (U^i_{j1} - U^i_{j2})$$

where V^i is the votes i gives in the comparison of alternatives $j1$ and $j2$.

$$V^* = \sum_{i=1}^{n} V^i$$

so that V^* = the outcome in a vote between alternatives $j1$ and $j2$. There is, then, a j by j matrix of V^*, representing the outcome of every pairwise vote. The policy forecast is the alternative that defeats all other alternatives in pairwise head-to-head voting. In technical language, the social choice is the alternative for which it is true that every V^* involving that alternative has a positive value if that alternative takes the position of $j1$ for each calculation of V^i. This forecast outcome is the Condorcet winner and occupies the weighted median voter position.[11]

MEASUREMENT OF THE VARIABLES

For most issues it is possible to define a continuum, as presented in figure 2.7, that has clearly specified endpoints which encompass all of the possible resolutions of an issue in question. Assume that all feasible outcomes lie between the most extreme positions taken by groups within the society. Each group can be placed on the continuum at the position that represents its most preferred outcome, which approximates group *ideal points*. Each group's ideal point is compared with that of each other group. As previously explained, correlating these rankings of preferences shapes the first building block of the utility functions. For each actor i, the correlation between i's ordering of possible outcomes and j's ordering for possible outcomes is the value of U^i_j. The values reported in table 2.1 and derived from figure 2.7 depict the respective U^i_j scores from the hypothetical example.

The utility functions are created by transforming each U^i_j score to yield indicators of the value, or utility, associated with success, failure, and the status quo. We estimate utility functions by merging risk-taking propensities with preliminary estimates of "utility." Put another way, when the measure of differences in preferences is transformed to include risk, the quotation marks may be removed from the word *utility*.

RISK

The incorporation of orientations toward risk-taking is critical to the model since it embodies the way different individuals view the world. Two people, each confronted with the true probability of success and failure at roulette, may choose entirely different courses of action: one may gamble away his or her life's savings while the other refuses to play at all. The gambler is risk-acceptant, the other risk-averse. The willingness to take risks reflects one's relative assessment of the worth of success as compared to the cost of failure. For instance, some people abhor their circumstances so much that they are willing to gamble on the possibility of an even worse fate in exchange for a small chance to improve their lot. Others, valuing their current situation a great deal, are likely to be very cautious about risking what they already have in exchange for a chance for some improvement which they value only slightly.

The propensity to take risks can have an important impact on the settlement of an issue in dispute. It may make a major difference if one is risk-acceptant, risk-averse, or risk-neutral (i.e., willing to accept a fair bet) in determining the importance of winning a given issue. How can any party's willingness to accept risk be ascertained? Ideally, leaders might declare their initial policy positions precisely at their most preferred alternative on a given issue continuum. But this placement may not be most advantageous. Why not? Because the most extreme or isolated stance on an issue might require an equally heavy commitment of resources that is too costly for the group to bear (i.e., they may not have sufficient resources to win that position). Considerations of cost therefore encourage a more pragmatic approach, which takes the form of a less extreme or less isolated placement on the continuum. History is replete with martyrs who sacrificed their lives in pursuit of lost causes; likewise, others so fear defeat that they readily abandon their objectives, appeasing their foes rather than risking confrontation.

It is reasonable to assume that what a group perceives as feasible is never more extreme than what it ideally wants. Then, the U^i_j scores serve as temporary surrogates for utility. In any two-way contest, the group with the most resources is likely to win. Therefore, we define the proportion of resources possessed by one group relative to the total held by both it and its rival as the likelihood of success in a one-to-one dispute. Analogous combinations of capabilities serve to estimate the likelihood of success given support and/or opposition from third parties. Taken together, these indicators enable the calculation of a basic expected utility formulation.[12] Specifically, we compute here the solution to equation 1 from Appendix A under the preliminary assumption of risk-neutral behavior. We can, of course, substitute i's for j's and vice-versa. We define U_{sj} to equal the utility some group j attaches to defeating some other group i, with this value equal to $(1 - U^j_i)$. The value 1 denotes the utility j attaches to its own policies, so what it stands to gain is the difference between the value it attaches to i's current policies and the value it would attach to i's behavior if i adopted j's goals.

U_{fj} = the utility j associates with failing and being defeated by i. $U_{fj} = (U^j_i - 1)$

The probabilities of success are defined as relative proportions of resources:

$$P_j = [\text{Capabilities of } j/(\text{Capabilities of } j + \text{Capabilities of } i)]$$
$$P_{ik} = [(Cap_i + Cap_\kappa)/(Cap_i + Cap_\kappa + Cap_j)]$$
$$P_{jk} = [(Cap_j + Cap_\kappa)/(Cap_i + Cap_\kappa + Cap_j)]$$

Return to the earlier hypothetical example. Note that the likelihood of the GPL defeating Deng's supporters in a strictly bilateral dispute—if those supporters resist the GPL's demand for a policy shift by Deng—is only about .085 (GPL's political power = 4, Deng's = 43; therefore the probability of the GPL defeating Deng is 4/47 = .085). Now insert Deng's salience score of .10. (This score signifies the degree of Deng's interest in this issue, which defines for us the likelihood that he will enjoin the issue.) Note that GPL's "utility" for the outcome supported by Deng is .66, so that the GPL's "utility" for success (U_{si}) equals $(1 - .66)$ or .34. A strictly bilateral contest with Deng yields the following risk-neutral expected utility, which is computed by filling in the values for the following equation:

$$E(U_{ij}) = S_j \times [P_i \times U_{si} + (1 - P_i) \times U_{fi}] + (1 - S_j) \times U_{si}$$

which yields

$$.10\ [(.085)\ (.34) + .915\ (-.34)] + .90\ (.34) = .28$$

However, GPL can expect assistance and opposition from other groups. Thus, they expect the dispute to become multilateral, with the marginal contribution from each other group equal to the likelihood that that group will intervene multiplied by the group's marginal power in the conflict and by the "utility" each group is expected to contribute to each initial party in the dispute. To calculate these values we must solve the following equation:

$$E(U_{ik}) = S_k \times (P_{ik} + P_{jk} - 1) \times (U_{ki} - U_{kj})$$

Filling in the values for the four third-parties yields:

Ideologues: $.97 \times (.19 + .92 - 1)(.09 - [-.60]) = \quad .08$
Bureaucracy: $.97 \times (.43 + .95 - 1)(.14 - [-.54]) = \quad .25$
Army: $.15 \times (.23 + .93 - 1)(.60 - .94) \quad = -.01$
Modern military: $.15 \times (.26 + .93 - 1)(-.09 - .60) \quad = -.02$

Adding all of these scores (that is, the bilateral and the four multilateral expected values) yields an expected utility from challenging Deng of .58, which means that the GPL expects some policy gains from challenging Deng. Seeing that some benefit may be at hand, and assuming that Deng's policy is not expected to "improve" without a challenge, GPL has an incentive to try to alter Deng's position on the hypothetical issue.

Beyond the calculation of expected gains or losses from challenging, however, does a group face potential danger as a result of the position it takes? Would choosing a different policy posture leave it less or more vulnerable to defeat? Our notion of risk-taking is drawn from this possibility that a group can choose relatively safe or dangerous postures on public policy questions.

Group positions are conceptually seen as representing some tradeoff between what is really wanted and what is viewed as pragmatic. For any given issue, there is a range of vulnerability to which a group can be exposed. This means that there is some position the group can take that is least susceptible to defeat. This is the safest and hence most pragmatic position. On the other hand, the group could adopt a policy posture which would leave it most susceptible to defeat. This is the most dangerous position. Converting these intuitive ideas into expected utilities means that at the target group's safest position, the sum of others' expected utilities against it is minimized.[13] At the most vulnerable position the sum of expectations against the target group is maximized. The target group's actual position is necessarily associated with a sum of expected utilities against it that falls somewhere in this range. We define risk-taking to mean that groups who position themselves relatively close to their most vulnerable circumstance are more risk-acceptant, while those who position themselves near the minimum are more risk-averse. Those falling in the middle of the range are risk-neutral.

In technical language, we define each actor's security level as the sum of expected utilities held by opposition groups contemplating trying to alter the target group's behavior [i.e., $\Sigma_{j \neq i} E(U_{ji})$, which is simply the sum across all actors of the calculation illustrated in the above example]. The greater this sum, the more utility group i (the target group) believes its adversaries expect to derive from challenging it. As this sum gets smaller, some other group j is increasingly seen to be incapable of challenging i, and if the sum is negative, group i is in a position to extract concessions from j. One can identify the hypothetical policy position that would maximize group i's security level [i.e., $\Sigma_{j \neq i} E(U_{ji})$min] and the hypothetical position that leaves i most vulnerable to defeat [i.e., $\Sigma_{j \neq i} E(U_{ji})_{\max}$]. How proximate i's actual policies are to these extremes of vulnerability is taken as a reflection of group i's willingness to take risks. This risk-taking propensity is defined mathematically as

$$R_i = [2 \sum_{j \neq i} E(U_{ji}) - \sum_{j \neq i} E(U_{ji})_{min} - \sum_{j \neq i} E(U_{ji})_{max}]/$$

$$[\sum_{j \neq i} E(U_{ji})_{min} - \sum_{j \neq i} E(U_{ji})_{max}]$$

This term is then transformed to

$$ri = [1 - (R_i/3)]/[1 + (R_i/3)]$$

so that ri ranges between 2 and 0.5. This transformation is used to provide a convenient basis from which to introduce curvature into the utility functions. The division by 3, which restricts the range of curvature, is required to avoid possible division by zero. As ri gets larger, i's aversion to risk increases.

The utility for success and the utility for failure may now be fully defined. Both of these utilities are assumed to be functions of the similarity of policy preferences across actors, and the level of each actor's willingness to take risk. The utility associated with success is taken to be the difference between the value a group attaches to its most preferred outcome (defined as equal to 1.0) and the value it attaches to some other position, adjusted by the degree to which it is willing to accept risk. Likewise, the utility associated with failure is measured as the difference between the value attached to some policy alternative and the value attached to the group's most preferred outcome, adjusted by the risk factor. Thus, the potential for gain in a policy dispute is the ability to force others to accept one's position. The potential for loss is the consequence of being forced to accept the preferred position of some other group. The mathematics of each of these terms and how utility values change with risk-taking behavior are found in Appendix B at the end of this chapter.

We assume that winning, thus changing an adversary's policies for the better, equals or surpasses no effort to alter the adversary's current policies, given that those policies will continue unaltered if they are not challenged. In some situations, it may be better to accept existing policy rather than trying, but failing, to change it. With these assumptions and the definitions specified earlier, we have created utility functions whose curvature indicates that those who are fearful of risks tend to value "sure things" more highly than uncertain outcomes, while those who are risk-acceptant tend to attach greater value to risky endeavors. Appendix C at the end of this chapter details the precise effects of these assumptions and definitions.

How likely is an opponent to refuse to give in to an initial policy demand? This likelihood can be measured as a function of how important the issue is to that actor. Drawing a continuum with a range from zero to one hundred (see figure 2.8), we ask specialists to locate each group on the continuum at the position that represents the importance or salience of the issue for the group. A score of 100 indicates that a group is prepared to expend all of its resources on the issue. Similarly, a score of 50 suggests a .5 probability that the group will resist a demand to capitulate on the issue. Each value between 0 and 100 corresponds to a number between 0 and 1, which represents the probability of resistance (S_j).

The probability that one group can defeat another in a bilateral contest is, as noted earlier, evaluated as the proportion of available power that one group can bring to bear against the other. The probability of success for i and for j, respectively, in a multilateral contest, is defined analogously. Thus, defining group i's power as Cap_i and j's power as Cap_j,

$$P_i = Cap_i/(Cap_i + Cap_j)$$
$$P_{ik} = (Cap_i + Cap_k)/(Cap_i + Cap_j + Cap_k)$$
$$P_{jk} = (Cap_j + Cap_k)/(Cap_i + Cap_j + Cap_k)$$

To recapitulate, four terms—similarity of preferences, willingness to take risks, salience, and capabilities (or power)—are the building blocks for calculating each group's expected utility for every other group's objectives and thus for the policy forecast. These expected utility values, in turn, may be mapped onto Cartesian graphs which provide a visual representation of the political dynamics surrounding policy decisions.

Through the application of a small number of assumptions about how people respond to choices, we have developed a comprehensive way to analyze politics and policy formation. But the model is not without limitations. Two particularly significant restrictions are that we assume issues are unconnected to each other and that we assume preferences trail off steadily as alternatives move away from a group's ideal point. The former assumption precludes investigating trades between groups across more than one issue. Future versions of the model will permit the simultaneous examination of two or more issues. The latter assumption greatly simplifies political reality by eliminating cycles in which alternative A is preferred by society to B, B is preferred to C, but C is preferred by society to A. Such cycles must be rare when utility, rather than ordinal preference, is assessed. Still, we should be aware that the model does not allow for this situation. A third, strictly empirical limitation is that we have not measured what a group anticipates policies will be if it does nothing. Instead, we assume it anticipates the continuation of existing policy. An additional limitation is that the theory as set out here provides an interpretation for each of eight octants in the Cartesian graphs, but does not permit subtleties of interpretation for different points within an octant. Ongoing research is eliminating this restriction.[14]

Despite these limitations, our theory is parsimonious, powerful, flexible, and subtle. The remaining chapters demonstrate that this theory contains broad practical value and applicability. They set forth analyses of the Sino–British negotiations over the future of Hong Kong. Apart from analyzing the international negotiations between Her Majesty's Government and the People's Republic of China, we also discuss the internal political negotiations and maneuvering that will determine how the Chinese government will interpret and enforce the agreement. Finally, we analyze domestic Hong Kong politics in the years of transition to 1997, when China recaptures sovereignty.

Beyond the important economic consequences of Hong Kong's return to China, this issue contains the seeds of future relations between China and Taiwan and more than likely will affect China's overall international relations. The substantive topic we have chosen permits an especially good test of our theory. After all, parts of what we have forecast have since been resolved, but the forecasts extend to the end of this century and beyond.

We have provided a method that joins the detailed knowledge of experts with the explicit rigor of formal models. While individual experts might reach analytic conclusions equivalent to those arrived at through the use of a formal theory, the "value added" of our approach is that it provides even nonexperts with an efficient and effective means of reaching their own "expert" judgments.

Mathematical Appendix

Appendix A:
Expected Utility Model of Process

The formulation is:

(1) The Challenger's Welfare

$$E^i(U_{ij}) = [S_j(P_i(U^i_{si}) + (1 - P_i)(U^i_{fi})) + (1 - S_j)U^i_{si} +$$

$$\sum_{k \neq i,j} [S_k(P_{ik} + P_{jk} - 1)(U^i_{ki} - U^i_{kj})']] - U^i_{qi}$$

(2) The Challenger's View of the Opponent's Welfare

$$E^i(U_{ji}) = [S_i(P_j(U^i_{sj}) + (1 - P_j)(U^i_{fj})) + (1 - S_i)U^i_{sj} +$$

$$\sum_{k \neq i,j} [S_k(P_{ik} + P_{jk} - 1)(U^i_{kj} - U^i_{ki})']] - U^i_{qj}$$

(3) The Opponent's Welfare

$$E^j(U_{ji}) = [S_i(P_j(U^j_{sj}) + (1 - P_j)(U^j_{fj})) + (1 - S_i)U^j_{sj} +$$

$$\sum_{k \neq i,j} [S_k(P_{ik} + P_{jk} - 1)(U^j_{kj} - U^j_{ki})']] - U^j_{qj}$$

49

(4) The Opponent's View of the Challenger's Welfare

$$E^j(U_{ij}) = [S_j(P_i(U^j_{si}) + (1 - P_i)(U^j_{fi})) + (1-S_j)U^j_{si} +$$

$$\sum_{k \neq i,j} [S_k(P_{ik} + P_{jk} - 1)(U^j_{ki} - U^j_{kj})']] - U^j_{qi}$$

$E^i(U_{ij}) = i$'s perception of the difference in i's expected utility from challenging j's policies and from leaving j unchallenged; that is, i's expectation of its net benefit (or loss) from challenging j.

$E^i(U_{ji}) = i$'s perception of the difference in j's expected utility from challenging i's policies and from leaving i unchallenged.

$E^j(U_{ij})$ and $E^j(U_{ji})$ have analogous interpretations, but from j's perspective.

S_i = the probability i will resist a demanded policy change. S_j is the analogous term for j.

S_k = the probability that third party k will intervene in the dispute between i and j.

P_i = i's probability of succeeding in a bilateral contest with j. P_j is j's probability of defeating i in a bilateral contest.

$(P_{ik}+P_{jk}-1)$ = the marginal effect of third party k on the probability of i or j succeeding. This, and the associated utility terms, represents the algebraically reduced form of two lotteries, one in which k is assumed to join i, and one in which k is assumed to join j. Since, on balance, these are mutually exclusive alternatives (as are, for instance, i's decision to select the strategies of challenging or not challenging j), the net impact of these two lotteries represents k's marginal effect. That $(P_{ik}+P_{jk}-1)$ is the marginal contribution of k to the probability of success by i or j is easily shown. $P_i + (1-P_i) = 1$. Let P_j (the probability that j succeeds in the bilateral contest) $= (1-P_i)$. $P_i \leq P_{ik}$ since P_{ik} = the probability i succeeds given support from k. Similarly $P_j \leq P_{jk}$. Thus, since $P_i + P_j = 1$, $[P_{ik} + P_{jk} - (P_i + P_j)]$ must be the contribution of k.

U^i_{ki} = the value i believes it gains from support from k. U^i_{kj} = the value i believes j gains from k's support.

$U^i_{ki} - U^i_{kj}$ = the net value i believes will be contributed by k to the contest between i and j. Analogous terms with j as the superscripted actor refer to j's perception of k's value to i and j respectively.

The U_s terms refer to the utility of success for the subscripted actor as perceived by the superscripted actor in the event the subscripted actor challenges the relevant adversary in a bilateral dispute. Thus, U^j_{si} is j's perception of i's utility for succeeding in forcing j to change its policies to be in accord with i's wishes. The U_f terms are analogous to the U_s terms, except that U_f refers to the utility the superscripted actor believes the subscripted actor attaches to being defeated following its initiation of a bilateral challenge. These utilities are a function of the similarity in policies manifested by i and j, and of the risk-taking propensity of the superscripted actor.

U_q terms refer to the utility the superscripted actor perceives the subscripted actor attaches to no change in policy by its potential adversary. Despite the restrictive assumption that the relevant decision maker anticipates the continuation of its opponent's policies in the absence of a challenge, the risk-taking procedure that is introduced into the calculation of utilities preserves the existence of a distinct gambling threshold for each group in each situation. The expected utility associated with the no challenge option represents the relevant decision maker's gambling threshold. Thus, the expected utility from the option to challenge must exceed the expected utility from the no challenge option in order for a rational decision maker to choose to initiate a policy challenge.

Appendix B:
Definition of Utility Functions

With U^i_i being equal to the value i attaches to its own most preferred policy outcome, and with U^i_j being equal to the value i attaches to j's policies as a function of their similarity to the policies of i, we may define the utility for success and failure respectively as

$$U^i_{si} = 2 - 4\left[(2 - (U^i_i - U^i_j))/4\right]^{ri}$$

and

$$U^i_{fi} = 2 - 4\left[(2 - (U^i_j - U^i_i))/4\right]^{ri}$$

Similarly, we may define the utility actor i attaches to the policy changes by its adversary that i anticipates will occur in the absence of a challenge by i as

$$U^i_{qi} = 2 - 4\,[(2 - [\,(U^i_i - U^i_j)_{tn} - (U^i_i - U^i_j)\,_{to}]\,)/4]^{ri}$$

t_0 refers to the present, while t_n refers to the near-term future. If no change in policy is assumed, the above reduces to

$$U^i_{qi} = 2 - 4[(1/2)]^{ri}$$

All U^i_j terms refer to the degree to which i and j share common policy preferences. U^i_i terms equal the value i attaches to its own policies, which we define as being equal to 1.0. Once the risk-taking component is combined with these variables, the appropriate utility function is defined. The transformations by 2s and 4s preserve the original scale of numbers while avoiding the generation of imaginary numbers. Since ri can be less than 1.0, the absence of such transformation would mean that for negative values of, for instance, U_{fi}, no real root would exist. This problem is eliminated with the introduction of these transformations. In this study we assume that each group guesses that its rivals' future policies will remain unchanged. In subsequent research a more detailed assessment of anticipated future policies will be utilized.

Of course, the U_{sj}, U_{fj} and U_{qj} terms (with appropriate superscripts) are defined analogously. These terms vary as a function of whose estimate of expected utility is being calculated (i.e., who is the superscripted actor) by varying the risk exponent, so that, for expected utility equations with an i superscript, calculations are done as specified above. For equations with a j superscript, j's risk-taking propensity is used to estimate what j perceives to be i's value of success, failure, or no challenge in accordance with the equations delineated earlier.

Appendix C:
Illustration of Utility Curvature

The effects of our definitions on the structure of utility functions is seen clearly in the hypothetical examples depicted in figure 2.9.

Figure 2.9

The Effects of Risk-Taking on the Utility Functions

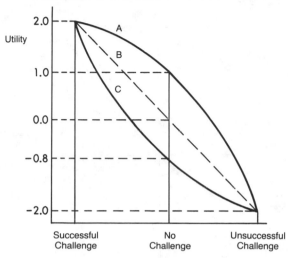

Possible Outcomes

Let the utility actors A, B, and C expect from successfully challenging j's policies equal 2.0. Similarly, let their utility for an unsuccessful challenge equal -2.0. Assume that a challenge will be successful with a probability of .5, so that the likelihood of an unsuccessful challenge also equals .5. Assume that if A, B, or C chooses not to challenge j's policies then the relevant actor believes that j's current policies will continue unchanged. Whether the risk of failure (.5) is too great for A or B or C depends on how much value each one attaches to the current status quo. To see how different the behavior of a risk-averse actor like A can be from that of a risk-acceptant decision maker such as C, examine figure 2.9. Note that for A the difference in value between the status quo and success is very small (the utility difference is 1.0), while for C the utility difference is very large. For C success has a utility of 2.0, while the status quo is valued at only $-.8$, meaning that living with the status quo is much less attractive to C than it is to A. Similarly, C sees little utility difference between failure and the current situation, while A

Figure 2.10

The Effects of Risk-Taking on the Multilateral Utility Function

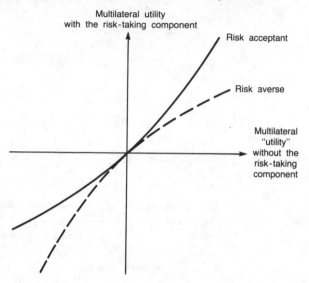

perceives a large utility difference. B, being risk neutral, falls in between these two extremes. The figure depicts the most extreme possible differences, given the way we have defined the risk component of the utility functions.

For the multilateral component of the expected utility equations, risk is introduced into the utility functions through the following transformation:

$$(U^j_{ki} - U^j_{kj})' = (U^j_{ki} - U^j_{kj})e^{Ri(Uki-Ukj)}$$

This functional form assumes that risk averters discount support from friends and inflate opposition from foes, while risk accepters inflate support from friends and discount opposition from foes. Figure 2.10 depicts the effects of the multilateral risk-taking function for risk accepters, risk averters, and risk-neutral decision makers, who fall in between.

3
Hong Kong: A Test Case

At the stroke of midnight on Monday, June 30, 1997, Great Britain's lease on the New Territories of Hong Kong, its sole remaining major colony, expires.[1] At that exact moment, all territory north of Boundary Street, along with several offshore islands now administered by Her Majesty's colonial government, revert to China. Hong Kong's largely Chinese population will watch with great apprehension the lowering of the Union Jack for the last time and the raising of the yellow five star on red flag of the People's Republic of China. Virtually every Chinese resident of Hong Kong is either a refugee from China or a first-generation child of a refugee.

Britain acquired Hong Kong Island as a port of access to the China trade under the 1842 Treaty of Nanking, which concluded Britain's victorious conduct of the First Opium War.[2] Following the Second Anglo–Chinese War in 1860, an additional three-and-three-quarters square miles of land—the peninsula of Kowloon and Stonecutter's Island—were ceded to Britain in perpetuity. Under the 1898 Convention of Peking, the New Territories, which cover just under four hundred square miles (over 92 percent of the colony's land area), were leased to Britain for ninety-nine years, which must have seemed an eternity to the colonial authorities. For more than a century following the

Opium War, Chinese nationalists protested foreign influence over sacred Chinese soil. By 1949, all vestiges of foreign dominion in China were erased, with the exception of the British Crown Colony of Hong Kong.

Since the 1950s, China's Communist government has taken the stand that the treaties ceding and leasing Hong Kong were "unequal," but that China alone would decide when this sole remaining historical foreign problem would be resolved. In 1972 it clearly stated to the United Nations Special Committee on Colonialism and Decolonization that Hong Kong's political status was an internal Chinese matter, and that it would settle the matter "when the time is ripe for negotiations." In the meantime, investors were repeatedly assured "to keep their hearts at ease," and the residents were told to acknowledge existing colonial authority in Hong Kong. It would not have been necessary for China to mount an armed assault to recover Hong Kong; a firm request to the British to leave, backed up by the threat to shut off food, water, and trade and otherwise harass the authorities and people of Hong Kong, would probably have sufficed anytime in the past few decades. Hong Kong as we know it is not economically viable without the New Territories, in which are located the bulk of its industry and water, the airport, and half its population. Since the Communist regime came to power in 1949, the Chinese and British have managed to coexist in peace and with mutual benefit.

As the 1980s approached, the live-and-let-live arrangement between Britain and China over sovereignty and administrative authority in Hong Kong gave way to increasing anxiety among international and domestic investors over the future of Hong Kong. To take but one example, how would banks structure domestic loans of fifteen years' duration after July 1, 1982, with no guarantees of contracts being enforced after July 1, 1997? The shrinking time horizon threatened to constrict investment and the future growth of the economy?

Sir Murray MacLehose, governor of Hong Kong between 1972 and 1982, seemed to enjoy especially good relations with the authorities in Canton and Beijing. In 1979 he became the first Hong Kong governor to visit Beijing in an official capacity. He was advised to take a message back to Hong Kong that "investors should put their hearts at ease," and that China had no intention of changing the status quo there.[3]

In 1982, Humphrey Atkins, minister of state at the Foreign and Commonwealth Office, visited Beijing, where he raised the issue of the expiration of the New Territories' lease with Premier Zhao Ziyang.[4] The Hong Kong business community, both local and international, had pressed the Hong Kong government to find out what China had in mind for the post-1997 period. Atkins pointed out that, according to the act of Parliament concerning the lease, the British government's authority over the New Territories would cease on July 1, 1997.

British Prime Minister Margaret Thatcher was scheduled to visit China on September 23, 1982, and on her agenda was discussion of the future of Hong Kong. In consultation with Foreign Office experts and Hong Kong government officials, she prepared a position to be put forward at the talks with Beijing's top leaders. Apparently overruling her advisers, she infuriated Chinese leaders by insisting on the validity in international law of the three treaties ceding and leasing the various components of Hong Kong to Britain. After all, she argued, how many countries have national boundaries that are wholly unaffected by prior conflicts? Having just successfully concluded a war with Argentina defending British sovereignty over the Falkland Islands, she was in no mood to concede sovereignty over Hong Kong to China.

In response, the Chinese government declared its intention to assert its sovereign right to control the whole territory of Hong Kong no later than July 1, 1997. The first round of diplomatic talks on the future of Hong Kong was held in Beijing in early October 1982. Talks continued throughout 1983 and 1984 against the backdrop of China's warning that it would impose a unilateral solution if a negotiated agreement for the transfer of sovereignty and administrative authority over Hong Kong were not reached by September 1984.

To see what was at stake in the Sino−British negotiations requires a clear understanding of the political economy of Hong Kong, the benefits that both China and Britain have derived from Hong Kong, the two nations' respective concerns over the outcome of the negotiations, the major issues to be resolved, and the impact on the international community of the potential transfer of sovereignty and administrative authority to China.

A TEST OF THE EXPECTED UTILITY MODEL

The Sino–British negotiations over the future of Hong Kong provide an excellent test case for the expected utility model of political analysis and policy forecasting developed in chapter 2. The policy changes emerging from these negotiations reflect the interests and resources of relevant actors in Great Britain and the People's Republic of China, as well as interest groups inside Hong Kong that can exert influence on the two main parties. Neither nation is a decision-making monolith; decisions reflect the contending interests and varying resources of a variety of relevant groups within the two nations. As we shall see in detail in chapter 4, China's leader, Deng Xiaoping, must contend with such internal groups as Communist Party ideologues who do not share his pragmatism and obsession with economic modernization, conservative bureaucrats who attained positions of importance before Deng's rise to power, two rival factions in the Chinese military, and the regional interests centered in Guangdong Province, adjacent to Hong Kong. The British government, in turn, must take into account the concerns of several business groups with interests in Hong Kong and the China trade.

The policy changes that emerge from the agreement will also have an impact on the international community, including Hong Kong's main trading partners and its memberships in international agreements. Thus the negotiations over Hong Kong's future illustrate international as well as domestic decision making, providing a test of the versatility and range of the expected utility approach. Finally, the Hong Kong negotiations provide an excellent opportunity to apply the expected utility approach to a very important problem—the future of a densely inhabited territory numbering more than five million people. This study forecasts the principles of an agreement reached in 1984, along with changes in the interpretation and implementation of the agreement as 1997 approaches. It also predicts the changes that will take place within the colony from now until the formal transfer of sovereignty, and post-1997 policies under Chinese rule.

The Sino–British negotiators addressed a raft of economic, political, legal, and social questions. Issues include changes in Hong Kong's free market system of economic organization, future administrative or constitutional links with Britain, the renewal of land leases, the independence and convertibility of the Hong Kong dollar, guarantees of civil rights, independence of the judiciary and the retention of the English common law system, restrictions on travel to and from Hong Kong, pension guarantees for Hong Kong civil servants, the language to be used in Hong Kong schools, the stationing of troops from the People's Liberation Army in Hong Kong, free elections within Hong Kong for local officials, and the right of pro-Taiwan organizations to operate freely. Taken together, the cumulative resolution of these specific policy issues and others will determine Hong Kong's future political and economic environments. Thus, many individual policy choices, each important in its own right, play a part in setting the framework for the overarching issue of the future status of Hong Kong. Political instability or disorder need not be a consequence of revolutionary change, but can occur as a result of normal political interaction over a broad range of concrete issues.

THE POLITICAL ECONOMY OF HONG KONG

No sharper contrast in economic policies and economic performance can be found than in the side-by-side comparison of the incredibly successful record of Hong Kong's free market economy and the dismal results of the command and control system of economic management employed by its colossal Communist neighbor. On a visit to London on May 10, 1984, a delegation of unofficial (nongovernmental) Chinese members of Hong Kong's Legislative and Executive Councils issued a statement reflecting their deep concern about Britain's handling of the talks with China over the colony's future. Expressing disappointment at the prospect of Chinese sovereignty over the territory after 1997, their statement bluntly maintained that "the inescapable fact is that the Chinese government is committed to a political philosophy which is at least incompatible, and at worst hostile, to the philosophy on which the various systems and freedoms enjoyed by Hong Kong today rest."[5] In particular, these leading members of Hong Kong's Chinese community were seeking assurances that the restoration of Chinese sovereignty would not alter Hong Kong's existing social, economic, and political systems, which have evolved on the basis of a constitutional link between Britain and Hong Kong that extends back more than 140 years.

Hong Kong is widely regarded as the industrial world's single best example of the free market economy model of development.[6] Throughout its history, Hong Kong has had to overcome many obstacles and has received almost no foreign aid in the process. Its land area is virtually resourceless, consisting largely of unproductive granitic rock formations. It ranks among the world's most overpopulated areas and is dependent on imports for the bulk of its food and raw materials, and all capital equipment. Located thousands of miles from its most important markets, Hong Kong historically has been unable to control population movements across its borders. To this day, it continues to be ruled by a colonial government that critics regard as obsolete, antiquated, and inconsistent with the principles of independence and self-rule. Yet despite these formidable obstacles, the rate of growth of the Hong Kong economy was so rapid in the post-World War II era that it began to seem almost inevitable. And despite its anachronistic colonial administration, a secret-ballot referendum among Hong Kong's residents would, in all likelihood, produce a near-unanimous vote of no confidence in the restoration of Chinese sovereignty and an equally strong preference for an indefinite extension of the status quo under British rule.

The British physically occupied Hong Kong in early 1841, a year and a half before the Treaty of Nanking, signed on August 29, 1842, legally transferred sovereignty and administrative control to Her Majesty's Government. By the end of 1841, the population of Hong Kong was estimated at about fifteen thousand, the great majority of whom were Chinese people of the surrounding region, attracted to Hong Kong for its employment and commercial opportunities despite the prevalence of tropical diseases there. Captain Elliot, the de facto administrator of Hong Kong, announced that its Chinese residents would enjoy British protection, but would be governed by traditional Chinese law. Trade would be free of tariffs. The Manchu government of China had discouraged and even forbidden the emigration of Chinese overseas. But this decaying dynasty was unable to enforce its edicts. Large numbers of Chinese continued to move into Hong Kong and through it to Southeast Asia, America, and elsewhere around the globe.

Throughout most of its history, Hong Kong has willingly accepted political refugees and immigrants seeking freedom and opportunity. Several hundred thousand such people entered Hong Kong in the 1930s during the Sino–Japanese War. Later, during their World War II occupation of Hong Kong, the Japanese forcibly deported large numbers of Chinese to China in order to ease the local food shortage. Four years of Japanese rule reduced the population of Hong Kong to about one-third of its prewar size of 1.8 million. But after Hong Kong's liberation from the Japanese in 1945, the deported Chinese returned at a rate approaching one hundred thousand a month, and by the end of 1947, the population had regained its prewar size. Still another influx took place during the Chinese civil war of 1948 and 1949, when nearly half a million people, mainly from Kwangtung (Guangdong) Province, Shanghai, and other commercial centers, entered the colony. Thus, aside from returning residents, immigrants increased the population between 1945 and 1956 by approximately one million, of which seven hundred thousand were refugees. Another flood of people crossed the border in 1962, following three years of bad harvests in China. Several hundred thousand Chinese entered during 1979 as the Cultural Revolution wound down; simultaneously, sixty-five thousand "boat people" from Vietnam, mostly ethnically Chinese, landed in Hong Kong.[7] The 1981 census showed that 98 percent of the population were ethnically Chinese and that 57 percent were born in Hong Kong. Thus, virtually ever Chinese resident of

Hong Kong is either a refugee from China or a first-generation child of a refugee.

How did Hong Kong's economy fare under an inundation of poorly skilled, badly educated immigrants? Until 1982, Hong Kong enjoyed a steady pattern of remarkable economic growth under a regime of liberal economic policies and a conservative fiscal policy. In 1948, per capita income in Hong Kong stood at US$180. Hong Kong's postwar transformation was so dramatic that per capita income reached US$6,000 by 1982, a more than sevenfold increase in real terms (despite the uncontrollable population increases).[8] Real gross domestic product (GDP) grew about 7 percent per year from 1948 to 1960, accelerating to an annual average of 9 percent between 1961 and 1981. Productivity growth averaged 8 percent during the 1970s; the unemployment rate has remained below 3 percent, absorbing the population inflows; and capital formation (savings as a share of GDP) exceeded 20 percent throughout the 1960s and 1970s. Hong Kong's economic transformation occurred without foreign aid or special concessions to overseas investors.

In sharp contrast with Communist China's socialist economic system, economic affairs in Hong Kong are conducted in a free enterprise environment; individual workers, businessmen, and investors can pursue their own self-interest as they see fit. In short, Hong Kong's economic policy is one of nonintervention and minimal regulation.

Let us examine some specifics of this market-disciplined, free-enterprise economy.[9] Hong Kong's economic and tax policy does not discriminate between residents and nonresidents; in Hong Kong overseas investors may fully own local factories, banks, and other businesses. Hong Kong is a duty-free port and allows the entry and exit of most raw materials, consumer goods, and commodities, which means that Hong Kong manufacturers can supply both local and foreign markets on the basis of least-cost production. Free entry is permitted, indeed encouraged, into almost every line of production. No protection or government assistance is traditionally given to manufacturing industries, utilities, service industries, or private citizens. Market forces are allowed to shape both the economy and the labor markets. Hong

Kong does not impose a statutory minimum wage. Earnings of industrial workers fluctuate with overall economic activity, rising most rapidly during sustained boom periods. Trade unions play little part in setting wages or working conditions. Conservative fiscal policies have accompanied liberal economic ones. The government has adhered strictly to the twin aims of low taxes and balanced budgets.[10] Financial authorities in Hong Kong have consistently stressed one tenet of tax policy: low standard rates of direct taxation stimulate investment and facilitate economic growth. In Hong Kong, low tax rates have been consonant with budget surpluses, not deficits. In thirty-two of the thirty-five years through 1982, the budget ended the year in surplus, and interest earnings on the accumulated surpluses have become a major revenue item. (The world recession of 1982 and the political shock accompanying the September 1982 announcement that China would reclaim sovereignty in 1997 have contributed to the first string of deficit budgets in Hong Kong's postwar history.)

The government tries to operate its economic services on a commercial basis where possible. Once it has determined that it must supply a service to achieve social or economic objectives, either because the services are not provided by the private market or because there are common resources that only the public sector can provide (e.g., water supplies), it tries to conduct these public enterprises with minimum cost to the general taxpayer, relying on user fees and charges that reflect the market value of the goods or services provided.

In keeping with the economy's internal freedom, Hong Kong is a completely free market in money. No barriers restrict exchange between the Hong Kong dollar and other currencies. Hong Kong is today a major financial center and also has the third largest gold market in the world.

How has the common worker fared under this economic system? The evidence on postwar income distribution suggests that the 70 percent of the population in the third through the ninth deciles have gained the greatest share of the increase in total national income.[11] Low-paid unskilled workers benefited most from the rapid increase in employment opportunities. The well-being of the poorest fifth of the population has shown dramatic improvement: by 1976, their average household income reached US$1,300, which surpassed the poverty index of all other Asian countries. Low-income households pay little in income taxes. A family of four does not pay income tax unless it earns more than US$11,000. Indeed, only 218,000 salaried workers of a total population exceeding five million paid any income tax in the 1982 tax year. Moreover, 13,000 taxpayers, about 6 percent of the total number in the tax net, contributed over half the total yields from the salary tax, despite the low standard rate.[12]

From the end of World War II through July 1982, Hong Kong enjoyed remarkable political and economic stability, which has fostered prosperity without much internal pressure for the welfare state or outside intervention. What made this stability possible? One answer is found in Hong Kong's political geography. Hong Kong's prosperity has served the developmental interests of mainland China, largely through China's foreign exchange earnings from doing business in and with Hong Kong. Entrepreneurs from Britain and other countries also benefit from commerce in Hong Kong. Finally, the local residents, many of them refugees from China, have found in Hong Kong opportunity for personal economic improvement. Thus a tripod of consent—Britain, China, and the local population—has fostered this haven of economic success.

Second, Hong Kong's lack of economic resources necessitates its heavy dependence on external trade. This open economic structure restricts the range of productive intervention: the government can do little to alter the cost/price structure of exports or imports to the benefit of Hong Kong. This fact alone encourages a hands-off attitude on the part of government toward the private sector, though other developing countries in similar circumstances have been less inclined to follow Hong Kong's policy.

Prospective Chinese sovereignty over Hong Kong not only threatens Hong Kong's free enterprise economy, it also portends serious erosion of Hong Kong's civil liberties and social practices. Despite its colonial government and the absence of parliamentary democracy, Hong Kong citizens enjoy a wide variety of freedoms found in Western democracies: freedom of speech, press, assembly, travel, religion, employment, education, and lifestyle, rule of law, and private ownership of property. These individual freedoms are also embodied in the Constitution of the People's Republic of China; however, Article 51 provides for circumstances in which these freedoms may be disregarded. It states, "The exercise by citizens of the People's Republic of China of their freedoms and rights *may not infringe upon the interests of the state*, of society and of the collective, or upon the lawful freedoms and rights of other citizens" (emphasis added). So the 1997 transition means more than just a change in Hong Kong's free market economy. It also threatens major changes in the colony's legal, administrative, and social systems, challenging the rights of some 2.6 million British Dependent Territory citizens, mostly Chinese, who fear losing the protection of the British Crown.

Although the specter of 1997 has always loomed on the horizon, the live-and-let-live mutually profitable relationship between China and Hong Kong held out the possibility, however slight, that the status quo might be allowed to continue past the expiration date on the New Territories' lease. In the postwar era, Hong Kong provided China with badly needed foreign exchange, a window to the West, access to modern technology, and other economic benefits. After all, China could have recovered Hong Kong any time after 1949, as the saying goes, for no more than the price of a telephone call from Beijing. The September 1982 announcement from Beijing that China definitely intended to reclaim sovereignty over the whole of Hong Kong by 1997 once and for all ended any hopes of the status quo continuing into the twenty-first century. The maintenance of Hong Kong's prosperity, stability, and freedoms after 1997 will depend on China's sufferance, not British administration.

Although the worldwide recession hit Hong Kong's exporters earlier in 1982, Beijing's September announcement shattered political confidence in Hong Kong's economic future. Despite promises by Chinese authorities that Hong Kong's free-wheeling economy would not be integrated into China's socialistic, state-directed system, the stock, property, and foreign exchange markets went into a virtual free-fall. Asset values on the stock exchanges fell by one-third within a few months, and land values in the choice sections of Hong Kong Island and Kowloon fell to as low as one-fifth of their pre-announcement 1982 prices. The floating exchange rate that had been in effect since 1974 fell from HK$6.20 to US$1 in mid-1982 to a low of HK$9.55 to US$1 on September 24, 1983, until the government linked the Hong Kong dollar to the U.S. dollar at a fixed rate of HK$7.80 to US$1, requiring that new issue of Hong Kong bank notes be backed by equivalent U.S. dollar reserves.[13] The crisis also forced the government to depart from its traditional laissez-faire policy when it temporarily took over the Hang Lung Bank to ward off failure and further loss of confidence in the banking system.

The Hong Kong economy has remained on shaky ground since political confidence was shattered in September 1982. The financial secretary has presided over back-to-back deficits, each exceeding HK$3 billion. He was forced to raise the top corporate and individual tax rates by 2 percent, to borrow HK$1 billion from the local credit markets to reduce the deficit for the 1984–85 fiscal year, and to draw down a major chunk of Hong Kong's vaunted fiscal reserves. Land values have failed to recover. The stock exchanges have risen on bouts of optimism over encouraging statements from China only to retreat in inevitable despair when little progress took place in the Sino–British negotiations.[14] Despite a strong recovery in export orders throughout 1983 and 1984, new investment in plant and equipment has failed to materialize for the first time in Hong Kong's postwar history; in fact, real investment declined 8 percent in 1983 in an economy that has traditionally witnessed annual savings rates of 20 percent of GDP.[15] Investors lack confidence that Chinese authorities will preserve Hong Kong's free market economic system after 1997, and they have begun to transfer resources elsewhere.

On March 28, 1984, Jardine, Matheson and Company, Hong Kong's premier trading firm, which is literally synonymous with Hong Kong's founding and history, announced that it was setting up a new holding company in Bermuda to be the parent of the company's international business interests, including its Hong

Kong operations—a sort of reverse takeover.[16] Jardine's taipan, Simon Keswick, wanted to insure the firm's future operation under a British legal system. He bluntly explained, "When we are competing in the international marketplace, it is undoubtedly a disadvantage to have to deal with questions regarding the long-term future of Hong Kong."[17] Hong Kong share prices plummeted 61.76 points the day after, posting their biggest one-day slide since September 1983. China claimed that Jardine was acting in concert with the British government in an attempt to wring political concessions from China in the negotiations.

Another illustration of the no-confidence vote in Chinese rule emerged directly after a Hong Kong press conference held on April 20, 1984. Returning from Beijing following the completion of the twelfth round of talks, Sir Geoffrey Howe, Britain's foreign minister, extinguished any prospect of a continuing constitutional link with Britain after 1997. While noting that the British government was concerned to preserve the essentials of Hong Kong's legal, economic, social, and administrative systems, thereby preserving the people's freedoms, he said, "But it is right for me to tell you that it would not be realistic to think of an agreement that provides for continued British administration in Hong Kong after 1997."[18] In the next few weeks, the bellwether Hang Seng stock index fell another 150 points. The market gained several hundred points during the second half of 1984 as the outlines of the agreement became clear, thus reducing investors' uncertainty.

CHINA'S BENEFITS FROM HONG KONG

Why has a communist government in Beijing tolerated the existence of a foreign enclave on its doorstep for so many years— especially one that demonstrates the success of a free market economy in contrast with the disappointing performance of China's state-controlled socialistic system?

Economic benefits must rank first in this calculation. Since the mid-1960s, receipts from Hong Kong, now estimated at US$6 billion each year, have accounted for 30 to 40 percent of China's total earnings of foreign exchange.[19] To earn these large sums,

China supplies Hong Kong with about 20 percent of its imports, especially including a wide range of inexpensive consumer goods, oil products, the bulk of its food imports, and annually increasing quantities of fresh water. It buys less than it supplies, leaving a balance-of-payments surplus which helps finance China's development policies. In addition, Hong Kong is the clearinghouse for remittances to China. Local and overseas companies and individuals remit to their relatives and business associates upwards of US$100 million a year. Hong Kong also has the largest, deepest, and most modern port facilities along the China coast. It is an important center for distribution of goods made in China to the outside world. Each year, several hundred million dollars' worth of Chinese goods are exported through Hong Kong's port for destinations overseas. China's takeover of Hong Kong would not eliminate this economic benefit, except that the pace of port modernization would likely ease.

Apart from quantifiable economic and financial benefits, Hong Kong provides China with indirect but tangible benefits in the form of access to Western technology and modes of business management, a convenient center for trade contacts and financial negotiations, a training ground for thousands of Chinese technicians and service personnel, not to mention the opportunity for first-hand observation of the workings of a free market economy. Since 1949, and most especially since the advent of China's "four modernizations" campaign in 1978, Beijing has been experimenting with a variety of market incentives to improve the performance of its economy. The regime has much to learn from Hong Kong.

China's postwar relationship with Hong Kong has been largely one of economic pragmatism. Ideologically speaking, Hong Kong, a dependent capitalistic territory of a sovereign power on Chinese soil, should not exist at all. But China has allowed the British Crown Colony to exist and flourish because Hong Kong's prosperity has served its own interests. After all, China looks back on four thousand years of national history. Consolidating its power over the mainland and beginning the job of national economic reconstructuion after 1949 were more important tasks for the communist leadership than recovering Hong

Kong. The half century to 1997 is just the blink of an eye on the Chinese time horizon. Why not let the British administration and people of Hong Kong develop the most modern city in Asia outside Japan? It would, sooner or later, fall into Chinese hands.

BRITAIN'S BENEFITS FROM AND OBLIGATIONS TO HONG KONG

Apart from a few scattered tax-haven islands and Gibralter, Hong Kong is Britain's sole remaining major colony. The once majestic British empire, on which the sun never set, is no more. Since 1945, Britain's ministers have guided the colonies to independence within the Commonwealth, largely through the process of self-government. But pressure on the British to hand over independence did not arise in postwar Hong Kong, for several reasons. First, China has ruled out national independence for Hong Kong as a feasible political option. In addition, a large proportion of Hong Kong residents are refugees from China. Most refugees, seeking comfort and security, are predisposed to political quietism. Since most Hong Kong residents have presumed that their future would be determined by ministers in London and Beijing, they felt there was little scope or point to local political activism. The only two serious political options have been the maintenance of some form of British colonial rule or a Chinese takeover. Therefore, most concentrated their efforts on getting rich, which is what life in Hong Kong is really all about.

What are Britain's benefits from administrative authority over Hong Kong? In the nineteenth century, it served as one of a string of British naval stations around the world that provided bunkering and repair facilities. This strategic era has passed and the naval dockyard has closed down. There is no British fleet in the Far East and the British base in Hong Kong is now an isolated outpost. What few forces remain, a contingent of British-officered Gurkhas, assist in internal security; they are not there to defend Hong Kong against external aggression.

Hong Kong provides Britain with modest economic benefits, which are concentrated in a handful of trading companies and individuals. In general, Hong Kong is not a captive market for

British goods, which compete with goods from other countries in Hong Kong's free market. Still, funds flow from Hong Kong to Britain in the form of pensions for retired Hong Kong civil servants living in Britain, dividends for British shareholders in Hong Kong firms, and payments for commercial facilities arranged through the City of London. British firms have provided Hong Kong's railways and rapid transit carriages. The nationalized British Airways Corporation gains from Britain's authority to negotiate landing rights at Hong Kong's airport. Britain grants landing rights in Hong Kong to other countries, in exchange for preferential foreign routes to British Airways.

Apart from the few concentrated interests in Britain that have a direct stake in colonial rule, the vast majority of the British public know little and care less about Hong Kong. Until 1984, media coverage in Britain on Hong Kong affairs was virtually nonexistent. Polls show that a majority of British residents are not aware that Hong Kong is a British Crown Colony. The public generally regards Hong Kong as host to sweated labor that competes unfairly with British textile producers.

Britain's experience with Caribbean West Indians, Pakistanis, and Indians has prompted it to lock the door on the sole large remaining class of overseas British passport holders. To discourage immigration, Parliament passed the British Nationality Act of 1981.[20] The act reclassified 2.6 million British passport holders, formerly known as citizens of the United Kingdom and Colonies, as British Dependent Territory citizens. Stringent rules of patriality disqualify virtually all such citizens from applying for British citizenship, which brings with it the right of abode in Britain. There is an escape clause for Crown servants in a dependent territory, but the British government has stated that this discretion would be exercised only sparingly. With the 1981 act, Britain effectively excluded its Hong Kong subjects from refuge.

Despite the apparent contradiction of the 1981 Nationality Act, British leaders have claimed moral responsibility for the people of Hong Kong. No British prime minister has wanted the responsibility of handing over five million people living in economic and personal freedom to the Chinese Communist Party.[21] It might have been easier to dispose of the colony if the local people had demonstrated any desire to live under communist rule. But Hong Kong's people have resisted Maoist blandishments even when they have been backed up by street agitation and occasional violence. Hong Kong residents should know what the choice involves. Several million were born in China and voluntarily sought refuge under colonial rule; several hundred thousand of them risked their lives to escape. Delegations of Hong Kong Chinese have repeatedly visited London to urge British ministers and members of Parliament to preserve the freedoms they have enjoyed under British administration. Under these circumstances, it has not been easy for Britain to abandon Hong Kong.

BRITISH AND CHINESE CONCERNS OVER THE FUTURE OF HONG KONG

Both sides agree on one point: each wants to preserve the stability and prosperity of Hong Kong in the transition years leading up to 1997 and following any changes that resumption of Chinese sovereignty entails. Surely China knows that kicking the British out of Hong Kong threatens the climate of business confidence which has been so essential to Hong Kong's postwar stability and prosperity.[22] The run on the Hong Kong dollar in the wake of China's threats in September 1983 vividly disabused the Chinese of any notion that British concerns might be ignored. Yet, for China, return of its sacred soil is required to restore national honor and erase the indignity inflicted by the British during the Opium War more than 140 years earlier. The Chinese do not wish to surrender benefits they derive from the colony's present status, but sustaining these advantages now plays second fiddle to the overriding political objective of reestablishing sovereignty over Hong Kong. It is one thing to wait for the scheduled expiration of a lease granted in 1898. It is quite another to grant an extension of sovereign authority to a foreign power on the basis of a series of three treaties that the regime does not recognize as valid. Although the British saw the existing treaties as the starting point for negotiations, the Chinese rejected any suggestion that these symbols of China's humiliation at the hands of British imperialism deserve serious consideration. If the price of sovereignty runs as high as economic collapse, Chinese leaders are prepared to pay it. But, in the best of all worlds, they would like to have their sovereignty and retain all of the economic benefits they currently enjoy.

To that end, apart from the two inalienable features of recovering sovereignty and administrative authority, China has stated its intention not to interfere in Hong Kong's internal affairs. The central government in Beijing would exercise responsibility for defense and foreign affairs, but in all other matters would allow Hong Kong people to rule and administer themselves, preserving their present way of life, including economic and personal freedoms. They have promised that Hong Kong would be allowed to retain its capitalist system for at least fifty years after 1997.

Since July 1983, China has waged a war of promises in trying to assure Hong Kong residents of its honorable intentions. The authorities in Beijing have spoken with many voices and through a variety of channels. The basic ten-point proposal that has provided the basis for China's guarantees about Hong Kong's future was first given to a delegation of the Hong Kong Federation of Students which visited Beijing in July 1983, and subsequently published in the pro-Communist newspaper, *Ta Kung Pao*.[23]

Hong Kong would be established as a special administrative region, in accordance with Article 31 of the evolving Chinese Constitution, which was revised for the fifth time in 1978. Apart from defense and foreign affairs, Hong Kong people will run their own administration. The Chinese government will not send officials to govern Hong Kong. Local people will choose their own mayors or administrative heads. They will make their own laws and retain all present laws save those that contradict Chinese sovereignty. (Under Article 51 the Chinese government can interpret sovereignty very broadly.) Hong Kong residents will enjoy freedom of the press, assembly, association, residence, and free entry and exit from the territory. Hong Kong will maintain its own police force. It will keep its capitalist economic system (for at least fifty years) and maintain its free port and world financial center.

Promises have also been made to delegations of Heung Yee Kuk (a New Territories representative body), *kaifong* (community) associations, and urban council and district board members (these comprise the bulk of the Colony's locally elected officials). Promisers include Ji Pengfei, head of the Hong Kong and Macau Affairs Office in Beijing, Xu Jiatun, head of New China News Agency in Hong Kong and better known as China's unofficial ambassador to Hong Kong, and the top echelons of Party and government officials.

In the short month following Sir Geoffrey Howe's mid-April 1984 visit to Beijing, Hong Kong people were promised that they could retain two passports, one British and one Hong Kong (Chinese); that while Chinese troops might be dispatched to Hong Kong to replace local British contingents, they would not interfere with local administration; that land leases in the New Territories would be extended after 1997 with cheap premiums; that Hong Kong's export quotas would be kept separate from those of the mainland; that Hong Kong could retain separate membership in such international economic organizations as the General Agreement on Trade and Tariffs (GATT) and the Multi-Fibre Arrangement; that it could have a separate ship registry; that it could establish its own central bank and maintain a separate Hong Kong dollar; that it could maintain commercial relations with Taiwan and other countries not having representation with Beijing; that the head of administration in Hong Kong, whether elected or appointed, will in turn appoint senior Hong Kong government officials and be answerable to the Chinese National People's Congress; that freedom of speech, travel, and press and the right to strike will be maintained; and that Hong Kong residents will be exempt from the military draft.[24] Many of these, of course, require foreign approval and are thus not in China's power to grant unilaterally. Other nations may refuse to recognize Hong Kong's semi-autonomous status once it reverts to Chinese rule.

Beijing has announced that it will draft a "mini-constitution" which it will introduce for the Special Administrative Region of Hong Kong under its Basic Law. They have promised to consult a wide spectrum of opinion in Hong Kong during this drafting process. But, put bluntly, the Chinese government's biggest problem in selling its position to Britain and the people of Hong Kong is credibility. Since September 1982, the various market-places in Hong Kong have voted no confidence with their dollars in Chinese guarantees that the status quo will continue. The Chinese Communist Party has frequently and at short notice changed its policies, sometimes completely reversing them. Many Hong Kong residents vividly recollect the regime's promises to Shanghainese merchants and businessmen in 1949 to honor their property rights, promises that were broken a few short years later when their businesses were seized without compensation. Many Hong Kong residents fear reprisals for having left China in the first place. Others have a deep-seated aversion to the institutions and methods of Communist government.

Promises to consult Hong Kong residents during the drafting of a "mini-constitution" for Hong Kong do not square with Beijing's earlier insistence that the Sino–British talks on the future of Hong Kong are bilateral. Prior to the second round of talks on July 12, 1983, the governor of Hong Kong, Sir Edward Youde, told a persistent reporter that "he represented the people of Hong Kong."[25] The Chinese Foreign Ministry replied immediately that Youde would participate in the talks as a member of the British government delegation, in the process refusing to grant an entry visa to Peter Tsao, head of the Hong Kong Government Information Services. China thereafter repeatedly declared that Hong Kong should not be represented separately at the talks, since the Chinese government already represented the interests of the territory's people.

Apart from the question of Chinese credibility, Beijing may require British support in selling the mutual agreement to the international community. At stake are textile quotas, an independent currency and passport, membership in GATT—in short, general acceptance of Hong Kong's modified semi-autonomous status under Chinese sovereignty after 1997. British refusal to cooperate in this effort puts Hong Kong's economic future at severe risk. To take but one example, 60 percent of Hong Kong's exports go to the United States and the European Economic Community. Manufacturing accounts for 25 percent of its gross domestic product and 40 percent of its work force. Loss of the textile quotas is potentially ruinous.

MAJOR ISSUES UNDER DISCUSSION

The Chinese government's stated policy on Hong Kong is to maintain its stability and prosperity (including the high standard of living), preserve its current social, economic, and legal systems, and grant self-administration to a local government that would enjoy both internal and international legitimacy. To implement these general principles requires that Hong Kong's current constitution, the *Letters Patent and Royal Instructions*, be replaced by the territory's designation as a Special Administrative Region under Article 31 of the Chinese Constitution.

These statements of general principles have failed to provide sufficient guarantees to local and overseas investors since the confidence-shattering September 1982 announcement. If the talks had broken down, for example, China would have had to follow through on its threat of a unilateral declaration. British refusal to sign on the dotted line would have been taken in Hong Kong as the beginning of the end, which even China does not want, because its economic benefits would be put at risk. For the status quo to continue, the agreement reached between Britain and China had to spell out the details on a broad range of major economic, political, and legal issues. Hong Kong's Chinese leadership wanted the British to insist that the "mini-constitution" for Hong Kong be enshrined in China's Basic Law before the agreement was signed and ratified by Parliament. The territory's indigenous leadership also wanted Britain to maintain a residual status in Hong Kong beyond 1997 to provide reassurance that the terms of the agreement will be kept.[26] The British were not able to satisfy these goals. In short, Chinese credibility requires full details of the proposed administrative, legal, social, and economic systems applicable after 1997, adequate and workable assurances that the agreement will be honored, incorporation of

the agreement in China's Basic Law, and guarantees that the
rights of British nationals (British Dependent Territory citizens)
will be safeguarded. As we show in Chapter 4, the British were in
no position to secure guarantees.

Economic Issues

Hong Kong's market economy differs radically from China's
socialistic, state-controlled system. Hong Kong people enjoy a
broad range of individual economic rights and proprietary interests, including ownership of property, free movement of labor
and capital, freedom to travel, the right to trade in any currency
and to own gold. The colony itself is a free port without duties
and tariffs; it possesses a fully convertible currency backed by
external assets, participates in several important international
trade conventions, and is free to set its own fiscal policy. In
contrast, the Chinese government determines who is admitted to
universities, assigns jobs, rations many commodities, restricts
travel, and severely limits individual ownership of property; in
short, it exercises enormous day-to-day control over the economy. China's controls are the very antithesis of Hong Kong's
freedom.

China is rich in resources. Hong Kong is not so well endowed. The future prosperity of Hong Kong depends on the
continuation of capitalism and a free market economy. This
requirement is based on the features of Hong Kong's economy:
the lack of natural resources, little heavy industry and food
production, the need to import its food and raw materials, the
lack of a sizeable domestic market, the need to derive maximum
efficiency from its labor forces, the maintenance of a competitive
edge over other Asian countries, and, most crucial, the need to
maintain business confidence, as the business community will
only continue to invest and take risks in Hong Kong if it is
confident that conditions remain conducive to making a profit.
To underscore this last point, the economic recovery that took
place in Hong Kong during 1983 and 1984 is unique in that, for
the first time in the Colony's postwar history, new investment in
plant and equipment failed to materialize, which is a reflection of

the loss of business confidence due to Hong Kong's political uncertainty. Indeed, much of the investment placed in Hong Kong since August 1982 has originated from China, making China coequal with the United States as the colony's largest overseas investor. Whether this investment reflects sound business judgment or the need to shore up the colony's sagging land and equity markets is uncertain.

A key feature of the colony's economy is the speed with which it adapts to its external trading environment. For this reason, all government decisions which affect the economy must continue to be made locally. Any reference to external authorities in Beijing would cause costly delays.

Hong Kong's fiscal policy is important in attracting investors. Its low direct tax rate on business and personal income has been a crucial element in sustaining high economic growth rates. Hong Kong's independent authority to determine its system of taxation, without the need to share receipts with Beijing, will interest all investors in Hong Kong. Separate retention of the government's accumulated fiscal reserves will help insure its autonomy and ability to finance public programs.

China's currency, the Renminbi, is not as hard as the Hong Kong dollar. Interest rates in Hong Kong, the cost of credit, are set by the forces of supply and demand in Hong Kong and international credit markets. The Exchange Fund, a public body, holds the external assets that back the linked rate. The government's use of these assets to guarantee the value and convertibility of the colony's bank notes is an important element in maintaining business confidence.

Modification of Hong Kong's free-port status would damage the ability of Hong Kong manufacturers to procure inputs on a least-cost basis and to compete effectively on world markets. Under the present colonial government, Hong Kong has a separate identity in GATT and the Multi-Fibre Arrangement. It has thus been able to negotiate and use substantial textile quotas. Abrogation of these arrangements would generate potentially devastating unemployment and economic disorder.

Unlike citizens of China, Hong Kong residents enjoy the right to travel abroad, which is essential to international business transactions. Internal freedom of travel also provides an incentive to Hong Kong's labor force to seek out the best wages and working conditions. If Beijing assumes immigration authority, controlling the movement of people in and out of Hong Kong, international business transactions could be severely limited.

Hong Kong's rapid economic growth has at times strained its infrastructure, which has struggled to keep pace with double-digit growth rates. The colonial government is staffed with a highly skilled, experienced workforce, well trained in tailoring infrastructure and services to the needs of a dynamic market economy. If these professionals choose to leave, they could not be easily replaced, either from China's own store of skilled workers or by contracting out to expatriates.

Some of these economic concerns are purely internal, requiring only that iron-clad guarantees be honored up to and after July 1, 1997. Other economic matters—quotas, travel documents, airline landing rights, trade agreements, currency acceptance, and defense agreements—require international cooperation. Unless the Hong Kong and foreign business communities can be persuaded that the Chinese will honor their promises and that international arrangements will remain in place, Hong Kong's future prosperity does not appear so inevitable.

Legal and Political Issues

The constitutional foundations of government in Hong Kong derive from the colonial regulations, which served as "directions to Governors for general guidance by the Crown through the Secretary of State for the Colonies."[27] The basic documents are the *Letters Patent and Royal Instructions*, which are elaborated in a multivolume set of *Regulations of the Hong Kong Government*. The constitution of the colony provides for executive and legislative branches of government, with an independent judiciary. But Hong Kong is not a representative democracy. Administrative and executive authority lie in the hands of appointed civil servants whose personnel, at the higher levels, have been recruited chiefly from Britain. Popular opinion, in the form of periodic elections to the Legislative Council, the colony's legislature, or public opinion polls, neither guides nor constrains Crown servants. The governor appoints prominent members of the community to the Legislative Council. Thus Hong Kong political activity has not reflected typical Western democratic practices of political party competition, the quest for votes, fighting over shares of the pork barrel, and extensive public debate of social issues. This is not to say that informed public views are wholly disregarded. The colonial government taps representatives from all segments of the community to serve on advisory committees and it floats "green papers" (draft policy proposals) for public discussion before enacting major new legislation. And starting in 1985, 24 of 56 Legislative Council members are elected.

These political circumstances have allowed a succession of governors and financial secretaries to practice financial integrity. Hong Kong has enjoyed total financial independence from London since 1958; throughout the postwar period it has continued to be fiscally sound, even as London and a host of former dependent territories lapsed into financial profligacy. The government has aggressively fostered localization of public services and introduced greater democratization in local government in the 1980s. The public at large elect officials to serve on the urban councils and the district boards; some elected board members, in turn, are appointed by the governor to sit in the Legislative Council, thus creating a form of indirect election to the legislature. At his April 20, 1984, press conference in Hong Kong, Sir Geoffrey Howe announced that "the government of Hong Kong will be developed on increasingly representative lines," thus beginning a process of creating a Hong Kong run by a Hong Kong people independent of expatriate skills by 1997.[28] One scenario would expand the elected urban council and district boards, which would then elect some fraction of members to the Legislative Council, which, in turn, might elect a majority to the policymaking Executive Council. Ultimately, Hong Kong people might, through further development of this process, indirectly have some say in the selection of the governor. The evolution of representative government in this manner looks forward to the creation of a locally governed going concern which would leave no vacuum for Beijing to fill as the British depart. Other scenarios could include direct elections of legislative and executive councillors, but these appear to be less likely owing to the need to maintain political stability to insure business confidence. Direct elections might foster open political conflict between Beijing-backed leftist groups in Hong Kong and pro-autonomy communities. Of course, Beijing's wishes will play a major role in the evolution of representative local government in Hong Kong. Will China dictate the course and progress of democratic reforms in Hong Kong? Will it insist on a veto in Hong Kong elections either before or after 1997? Will laws passed by the post-1997 legislature be subject to Beijing's approval? Apart from China's involvement in this process, will growing democratization bring pressures for spending programs found in other democracies, thus increasing taxes and jeopardizing the territory's attractiveness to investors?

The institutions of government also include the judiciary and legal system. The Hong Kong legal system rests on English common law modified slightly by traditional Chinese laws and customs. It is based on an elaborate mechanism developed over the centuries to protect the rights of the individual. The most important features of the common law system are its stress upon the rule of law, the existence of a judiciary free from the executive branch and other political pressures, reliance on precedence to insure consistent and predictable interpretation of the law, and recourse to the principles of equity to soften the rigidity of general rules of law. In Hong Kong, an aggrieved resident can sue the government and win. In China, no similar privilege exists.

Other legal matters include the language of the law, which in Hong Kong is English, and reliance on legal precedents set in Hong Kong or elsewhere in the Commonwealth. Many of the rules of interpretation and judicial definitions for words and phrases have evolved over the years and are foreign to the Chinese language. Since other Commonwealth cases bear upon Hong Kong's common law system, this could create problems should the Chinese insist on modifications in Hong Kong's legal system. The language barrier or misunderstanding of British common law could be especially serious if China sent its own jurists to occupy the highest positions in Hong Kong's courts. Under colonial rule, legal decisions of Hong Kong courts can be appealed to the law lords of the Privy Council in Britain. For example, local sentiment runs in favor of the death penalty for capital offenses, but, in the case of an appeal, Britain commutes any death sentence in keeping with British norms and practice. Appeal to the Privy Council is, of course, grossly inconsistent with the practice of Chinese sovereignty. What role, if any, will Beijing play in Hong Kong's court system?

It would be a mistake to believe that Hong Kong residents care only for their economic liberties and material benefits. They care equally for their noneconomic liberties. Under British constitutional and legal systems, Hong Kong residents enjoy such civil liberties as freedom of religion, speech, press, and assembly, including the right to criticize public policies. These freedoms, although enshrined in China's Basic Law, are perennially threatened under Article 51 of its Constitution. Will Beijing allow Hong Kong intellectuals to criticize mainland economic and political decisions?

Present land leases in the New Territories are scheduled to expire on June 27, 1997. Will the Chinese guarantee that holders can renew these leases under current financial terms? Fears that Beijing will tax leaseholders could stifle development in the New Territories, where most of the colony's industrial growth is scheduled to develop. What will be the legal status of all contracts in force on July 1, 1997?

Civil servants' pensions in Hong Kong are funded from appropriations in the annual government budget. To preserve the morale of the bureaucracy, post-1997 pension payments must be guaranteed. An offshore fund could insure pensions even for civil servants who are British nationals, but the Chinese might balk at the use of Hong Kong public funds.

Perhaps the single most sensitive political issue is the stationing of People's Liberation Army units in Hong Kong after 1997. After all, the British have garrisoned up to ten thousand troops in the territory and can scarcely insist that another sovereign nation not station troops on its own soil. On May 21, 1984, Geng Biao, vice secretary-general of the National People's Congress, said during its annual meeting, that Chinese troops would not be posted to Hong Kong. These remarks were quickly contradicted by Foreign Ministry officials on May 25, 1984, who quoted top leader Deng Xiaoping as saying that China will dispatch troops after restoring the exercise of sovereignty. Within an hour, a nervous stock market shed thirty points.[29]

Finally, will Beijing insist that Mandarin, the national language of China, replace English and the Cantonese dialect now used in Hong Kong's schools?

Impact on the International Community

International consequences immediately flow from the restoration of Chinese sovereignty.[30] For one, China is not a member of GATT, and even if it joins, it is not clear how other members would regard Hong Kong's new political status as a semi-autonomous Special Administrative Region in China. The same holds for the Multi-Fibre Arrangement, which insures Hong Kong textiles a major share of U.S. and European markets. Demands that textile quotas be renegotiated or, worse still, that Hong Kong's quotas be subsumed under China's, could devastate Hong Kong. Hong Kong's textile competitors may well view 1997 as an opportunity to carve up Hong Kong's quotas for themselves.

Another issue is Hong Kong's links with countries that have no diplomatic relations with China. Hong Kong's top twelve trading partners in terms of exports, imports, and re-exports include Taiwan, Saudi Arabia, South Africa, Singapore, South Korea, and Indonesia, none of which has diplomatic relations with Beijing. Should Hong Kong's official consulates in these countries be downgraded after 1997 to unofficial trade-promotion organizations or altogether canceled, it would impede travel from or to Hong Kong, thereby straining business dealings with these nations. At present, citizens of Malaysia, Singapore, and Indonesia are accorded free travel to Hong Kong, but their governments do not accord equally free travel to mainland China.

If these countries conclude that self-administration in Hong Kong is a façade, they may curtail the rights of their citizens to travel to Hong Kong and vice versa. Moreover, can China resist international pressures from North Korea and black Africa in order to permit continued consular representation in Hong Kong of South Korea, Israel, and South Africa?

A post-1997 Hong Kong passport would be a questionable travel document. Its validity will depend on other countries' accepting and recognizing a document issued by a nonindependent, semi-autonomous region of China. Even if the document is recognized in some countries, will its holders be accorded the same treatment that current holders of British passports issued in Hong Kong receive?

Hong Kong is Taiwan's third largest trading partner. Taiwan makes heavy use of Hong Kong for air and shipping links. Beijing already pressures the Hong Kong government not to allow pro-Taiwan rallies. After 1997, will it allow pro-Taiwan newspapers to continue publishing, permit the Taiwan-owned China Airlines access to Hong Kong, and allow pro-Taiwan organizations to maintain their operations? China has been making overtures to Taiwan, promising it autonomy over its economic policies and maintenance of separate armed forces if it agrees to surrender sovereignty to Beijing. Optimists for a successful post-1997 Hong Kong argue that China must honor its guarantees to the people of Hong Kong if it hopes to lure Taiwan back into the fold with a similar package.

British presence in Hong Kong technically makes Hong Kong a part of NATO, a condition that will change in 1997. British rule in Hong Kong has provided a stabilizing element in the increasingly important Pacific area basin in the form of a free international marketplace, a haven for rest and recreation for the American fleet and other friendly forces, an intelligence eye on China, a base from which to fight the traffic of drugs in the region, a key communications link, a free press, a free financial center, and so on. Any or all of these benefits to members of the international community of nations may disappear or erode depending on decisions taken in Beijing.

In the chapters that follow, we apply the model set forth in chapter 2 to Hong Kong's future. The main elements in those forecasts are, first, the major provisions of the Sino−British agreement for Hong Kong's post-1997 social, economic, and political future; second, the impact of internal Hong Kong interest groups' efforts to influence post-agreement developments in the Crown Colony's waning years; and, finally, how domestic politics in China will lead it to honor or erode the agreement after it has been signed, both up to and after 1997.

4
The Sino–British Negotiations: Issues and Assumptions

The model assumes that policy decisions are the product of competition among various groups on issues of concern. The actual resolution of a particular issue depends on three basic pieces of information which serve as data inputs into the model: the resources each actor possesses, the policy preference of each actor, and the importance of the issue to each one of the relevant political groups.

This chapter describes the issues and basic data inputs used in analyzing the future of Hong Kong. The first section provides a detailed overview of the three sets of major actors, which sometimes overlap, involved in the analysis. They are, first, those that influenced the Sino–British negotiations; second, those that can influence the direction of policies in Hong Kong between 1984 and 1997; and, third, those internal Chinese groups that can influence China's policies toward Hong Kong after 1997. The second section presents experts' estimates of the resources that the various actors can use to advance their policy goals. Several experts were consulted, each of whom has an outstanding reputation as a Hong Kong or China specialist. In the context of the international accords, a "base case" set of resource assumptions and two alternative scenarios are presented. Additionally, separate resource estimates are generated for the Hong

Hong and internal Chinese analyses. The third section graphically depicts the preferences of each actor and the salience each assigns to the issues.

IDENTIFICATION OF MAJOR ACTORS

The issues examined in this study can be grouped into three classes:

1. Issues relating primarily to the Sino–British settlement and the transfer of sovereignty, whose outcome was determined by a broad range of international actors.
2. Issues related to the day-to-day administration of Hong Kong, which will be increasingly determined by internal Hong Kong forces and growing mainland influence.
3. Issues whose implementation and determination will be increasingly influenced by domestic Chinese politics.

Analyses of all three classes of issues were completed in detail. An especially important set of results reveals the domestic political pressures on the Chinese leadership that are projected to play an increasingly important role with the passage of time. Indeed, Hong Kong's future will ultimately become dependent on internal policymaking in China. A separate analysis of internal British policymaking is unnecessary since British influence will steadily decline now that the negotiations have been concluded.

International Context

Experts' estimates about which groups will try to influence decisions, what outcomes they prefer, and how much clout they can exert are essential for defining the values on the variables contained in the expected utility models. The models' assumptions, then, drive the view of decision making that structures our variables and analysis, while the experts' information gives substantive meaning to those variables. The experts for this study identified ten major international actors involved in the Sino–British talks on the future of Hong Kong. Three represented direct British interests, three Chinese interests, three Hong Kong interests, and the remaining actor represented a combination of international observers. Within each cluster, one actor was dominant in terms of resources. The list of actors includes:

Chinese government (Deng Xiaoping)
Chinese military
Guangdong faction (southern Chinese)
British government (Margaret Thatcher)
Hong Kong Association (influential British firms)
British traders (firms doing business with China)
Hong Kong local business community
Hong Kong foreign business community
Hong Kong Executive Council members
The United States and other countries

The Chinese government. For the purpose of analyzing the international negotiations, the real political leader of China, Deng Xiaoping, represented all the key interests in China in the settlement of the Hong Kong issue. His colleagues in the Central Political Bureau of the Communist Party, including the premier, the head of the Chinese Communist Party, the foreign minister, the Office of Hong Kong and Macau Affairs in Beijing, the Chinese delegation to the Sino–British talks, and the director of the Hong Kong branch of the New China News Agency (the unofficial Chinese consul in Hong Kong) all spoke with one voice. All knowledgeable parties agreed that the Chinese negotiating team reported directly to Deng Xiaoping. Deng's instructions determined the Chinese position and China's willingness to accept the negotiated settlement.

The Chinese military. Hong Kong provides the best set of facilities available to the Chinese military. The harbor is the best along the entire coast of China, the international airport is first rate, and the colony's location provides a crucial communications link throughout the region. Top army commanders are regarded as politically to the left of Deng. To insure their support, he had to demonstrate his loyalty to the task of recovering China's sacred territory.

Guangdong faction. Historically, Hong Kong's ties with China have been handled via communist authorities in Guangzhou (Canton), the capital of neighboring Guangdong Province.

Most of Hong Kong's supplies of food, water, and other imports from China come by rail or truck from Guangdong Province. Border questions (bridges, roads, rail connections, and so forth) are negotiated with Guangdong officials. Thus southern China has the most direct experience in dealing with Hong Kong. Some southern Chinese believe that Hong Kong can aid the development of the region's economy. At present, China is experimenting with Special Economic Zone development in Shenzhen county, directly adjacent to Hong Kong. The bulk of investment in the Shenzen Special Economic Zone has originated from Hong Kong businesses. The authorities of Guangdong Province, therefore, wanted to settle the negotiations in a way that would further the development interest of their territory. Although they did not disagree with the leadership in Beijing about recovering sovereignty, Guangdong's unique concern is to utilize Hong Kong to suit southern interests, rather than seeing the benefits dissipated over the whole of China.

British government. The British government, under the leadership of Prime Minister Margaret Thatcher, represented the British side in the Sino–British talks on Hong Kong. The British government currently holds sovereignty over all of Hong Kong, including Hong Kong Island and Kowloon, until 1997 when the revocation of the 1842 and 1860 treaties takes effect.

A full picture of the British government includes the prime minister and her Conservative Party supporters, the Foreign and Commonwealth Office figures concerned with Hong Kong, the British ambassador to China (who headed the negotiating team), the governor of Hong Kong (who participated in the negotiations on the British side), and the political advisers to the Hong Kong government dispatched from the British Foreign Office. The combined views of this congerie of persons were represented through Margaret Thatcher.

As Britain's leader, Thatcher's views determine her government's position. On her instructions, the British negotiating team could have broken off talks, continued the talks without reaching any agreement, or consented to an agreement. The agreement that cedes sovereignty of Hong Kong Island and Kowloon to China also technically required the approval of both the House of Commons and the House of Lords in Parliament to revoke the 1842 and 1860 treaties.

Hong Kong Association. Throughout the history of Hong Kong, a handful of British trading firms have established a major position of economic power and influence in the economy. The most famous of these firms are Jardine, Matheson and Company (known as Jardines), Swire Pacific (John Swire & Sons), Hutchison Whampoa, and so on. The British offices of these Hong Kong–based trading firms have established an organization in Britain known as the Hong Kong Association (HKA) to represent their interests in the Colony. Their primary objective is to maintain their position of influence and privilege in Hong Kong's economy, which derives from more than one hundred years of major participation in the colony's development. In loose association with the HKA are several British firms that have large business contracts in supplying Hong Kong with railroad cars for the Mass Transit Railway and the Hong Kong–Kowloon Railroad.

British traders. Several British firms currently trade with the People's Republic of China and others are negotiating to join them. These business firms do not necessarily have major business operations in Hong Kong nor have they any plans to invest in Hong Kong. Their primary objective is to establish and develop growing links with mainland China. This group is not as well organized as the Hong Kong Association.

Hong Kong local business community. In some developing countries, overseas investors own half or more of all equity in business. In contrast, local Chinese predominate in the colony's investment portfolio. The great bulk of all new investment in plant, equipment, and real estate is undertaken by the local Chinese business community (though sometimes in partnership with overseas Chinese and foreign interests). Many of these businesspeople are immigrants from Shanghai and elsewhere in China and have already experienced confiscation of their assets in mainland China after the Communist Party came to power. The sharp collapse in the stock and property markets since 1982 and the failure of new investment to materialize throughout 1983 reflect the decisions of these important businesspeople. They are highly mobile and few would have any trouble in relocating their assets and residence abroad. If their confidence in the future of Hong Kong erodes, the prosperity of Hong Kong correspondingly dissipates.

Hong Kong Chinese businesspeople are not considered by Beijing to have the same standing as businesspeople from other countries. They are regarded as Chinese and will become subjects of China when it resumes sovereignty in 1997. Foreigners, in contrast, will remain nationals of their own countries after 1997, and therefore enjoy additional protection in their subsequent dealings with Chinese authorities responsible for Hong Kong.

For the settlement to be successful in maintaining the stability and prosperity of Hong Kong, it must appear credible to this group. The loss of this group's investments could not be replaced by any combination of new investment from foreign businesses or from China itself.

Hong Kong foreign business community. Foreign investment has played a major role in certain sectors of the Hong Kong economy, especially electronics, banking and financial services, and high technology. The United States is by far the largest overseas investor in Hong Kong, with substantial positions also taken by Japan, Britain, and other countries. These investors have been attracted to Hong Kong by its favorable business climate, strategic location, access to China, and regional importance.

Restrictions on the economic freedom these firms enjoy and any reduction in the colony's favorable business climate would adversely affect their interests. In addition, British firms with highly advanced technological processes, which are protected under British adherence to international patent and copyright agreements and property rights laws, might face some changes in their treatment under Chinese sovereignty. Increased investment in Hong Kong between now and 1997 might lead to preferential treatment from China after 1997; conversely, discrimination may follow if China regards any investment pullback as signaling no confidence in Hong Kong's future under China's flag.

Unlike the local Chinese business community, this group

need not fear nationalization of their assets, as their subsequent treatment under Chinese sovereignty is likely to be no worse than that presently accorded other investors in China.

Hong Kong Executive Council members. The Executive Council is the most important official political body in Hong Kong. The governor has a constitutional obligation to consult its members, who are appointed from the most important elements in the community, on all major matters of policy. He can constitutionally override their advice, but must inform British authorities in London whenever he does so. The phrase *Governor-in-Council* is used to mean a decision taken after the governor consults with his executive councillors. Each councillor takes an oath of confidence not to reveal any discussion, and each is encouraged to speak freely on matters of policy.

The Chinese members represented in some sense the interests of the local Chinese community. It was the policy of the British to inform the Executive Council about the negotiations and accept their advice. These briefings were minuted and gazetted. Prime Minister Thatcher indicated that the British would not reach an agreement with China that did not carry the approval of the Executive Council. The Chinese members thus had some form of potential veto over a settlement. This veto was weakened to the extent that they would risk bearing responsibility for an economic collapse and breakdown in law and order should their refusal to support compromise become known. These people are also highly mobile and could leave Hong Kong should they not wish to stay after 1997.

The United States and other countries. A number of countries have strategic and other interests in the future of Hong Kong as it might change under Chinese sovereignty. The United States government uses Hong Kong as a key intelligence outpost, a center for drug enforcement efforts throughout the region, a naval rest and recreation facility, and for other governmental services. The United States is closely allied with Britain but has been trying to strengthen its relations with China. The United States therefore hopes for an amicable resolution of the talks that allows it to maintain current benefits from Hong Kong and close ties with both countries.

Taiwan is also an interested party in the outcome and will

view the settlement of Hong Kong as a harbinger of its future dealings with the communist government in China. It is, however, a passive observer. Similarly, several other countries have consulates in Hong Kong and enjoy healthy trade with the colony but do not have official relations with China. Resumption of Chinese sovereignty may alter their beneficial relations with Hong Kong.

Internal Hong Kong Context

From the signing of an accord in September 1984 until the transfer of sovereignty in 1997, Hong Kong will enjoy thirteen years of diminishing British administration. Plans to increase the degree of representation in local councils are already in progress. What Hong Kong will look like when China takes over in 1997 depends on the scope and extent of internal changes during the colony's remaining thirteen years. To forecast these changes requires an identification of the relevant interest groups. Our experts identified ten major actors. Though neither the British nor Chinese governments appear as actors in this context, their interests are assumed to be represented by the expatriate civil servants and the leftists, respectively. The ten groups are:

Local political elite
Big local business
Small local business
British "Hongs"
Non–leftist workers
Expatriate civil servants
Middle–Level civil servants
Intellectuals
Leftists
International business

Local political elite. This group includes the Chinese members of the Hong Kong Executive Council and the Legislative Council, whom the governor has appointed to these positions. They are prominent businesspeople, professionals, educators, religious leaders, philanthropists, and so forth.

Big local business. This group includes the major local Hong Kong business interests in manufacturing, shipping, trading, services, etc. They collectively own the majority of locally held equities and property.

Small local business. This group consists of shopkeepers, sole proprietors, and small manufacturers.

British "Hongs". This group includes the major British business firms in Hong Kong such as Jardines, Swire and Hutchison. These companies have long historical ties to Hong Kong and are watched as bellweathers of international confidence.

Non-leftist workers. This group comprises the bulk of Hong Kong's apolitical labor force.

Expatriate civil servants. This group includes the governor and all major department heads and officials who are technically appointed by the Foreign Office on the governor's recommendation. Many have served in Hong Kong for twenty to thirty years. They are disproportionately British.

Middle-Level civil servants. This category includes all of the middle-level and professional ranks of the civil service and almost exclusively consists of local Chinese.

Intellectuals. This category includes university professors, students, journalists, middle-class professionals, and others interested and active in Hong Kong's newly developing internal political life. This group is likely to provide the new generation of indigenous political leaders.

Leftists. This category includes the New China News Agency, pro-communist unions, students, newspapers and other media, and leftist elements within the banking and business communities.

International business. Major firms owned by foreigners, excluding Hongs.

Domestic Chinese Context

In the context of Chinese domestic politics, our experts identified six major groups in China that will affect the future of Hong Kong. While this listing is more detailed than the three-group division presented in the international context, their general objectives are similar. The groups are:

Communist Party leadership
Bureaucrats
Communist Party ideologues
Modern military (air force, navy, missile)
Army (ground forces)
Guangdong Provincial leadership (GPL)

Communist Party leadership. Deng Xiaoping, Hu Yaobang, and Zhao Ziyang form the triumvirate leading the Chinese Communist Party. Deng is clearly at the pinnacle; Hu and Zhao obtained their positions through Deng's post-Mao shakeup of the regime. All three share a common interest in rejuvenating the Party and the government and oppose Maoist and Cultural Revolution radicals. Hu and Zhao diverge, emphasizing ideological concerns and bureaucratic politics respectively. Once Deng disappears from the scene, they may compete for primacy. At this time, however, there are no significant differences among the three of them on policies to be adopted toward Hong Kong.

Bureaucrats. The major segments of the vast Chinese bureaucracy share a common interest in economic modernization. This bears on Hong Kong's important role in generating foreign exchange, facilitating foreign trade, providing a reservoir of capital and managerial talent, and offering the opportunity for offshore oil exploration and exploitation. These considerations are of interest to various ministers and vice-ministers who are able to influence these policy questions, and of interest to others through their governmental positions in the State Council or their positions in the politbureau and the central committee of the Party.

Communist Party ideologues. This group consists of Maoists and other remnants of the Cultural Revolution, lodged primarily at the provincial and local levels of the Communist Party. Consisting of approximately forty thousand members, this group represents a potential for resistance to Deng's "compromises with capitalism," including his policies on Hong Kong. The Hong Kong question is one that this group might effectively exploit against Deng.

Modern military. The air force, navy, and missile brigades have received technological and monetary benefits from Deng's drive toward modernization. They now share a common interest in obtaining foreign technology for which Hong Kong serves as an important link. This group would also benefit from the continued flow of foreign exchange earnings required to finance purchases of dual technology and foreign weapons systems. Representatives of the modern military group rank high in the government and party organs.

Army. The People's Liberation Army ground forces pose several problems for Deng's modernization plans. Its leadership is generally older, less educated, and more dogmatic than the modern military faction. This group is strongly influenced by Maoist axioms and remains outside the post-Mao consensus fashioned by Deng. The Army generally identifies most with the preferences of the ideologues.

Guangdong Provincial leadership. The province of Guangdong adjoins Hong Kong and, as such, has a special interest in the colony. It has enjoyed greater independence from Beijing than other provinces, with the exception of Sichuan. In addition, remittances from and extensive trade with Hong Kong have enriched the province relative to the rest of China. As such, regional leaders have a vested interest in the future welfare of Hong Kong.

THE ACTORS' RESOURCE ENDOWMENTS

In performing these analyses, experts were asked to provide estimates of each group's ability to alter or affect policy. Often separate estimates of political, economic, and military resources are collected, thus permitting a more detailed examination of questions related to strategies groups can pursue. In the case of the Hong Kong negotiations, however, the experts indicated that military resources probably would not be employed to affect the set of issues under consideration. Furthermore, in their judgment, political and economic capabilities are so intermixed that an aggregate estimate of capabilities best serves the analysis. Thus, composite measures of overall influence were obtained for each actor for each forum: international, Hong Kong, and internal Chinese. In each case these measures were developed by first asking the expert to assign a score of 100 to the most powerful group. Then, the expert estimated the power of each other group relative to that of the most powerful group. For instance, an actor with a score of 50 must be viewed as having half as much power as the most powerful group. One with a score of 30 is three tenths as strong as the most powerful, and has six tenths the influence of a group with a score of 50. These scores, in turn, were converted into percentages. While this procedure reflects each expert's subjective estimates, their knowledge, coupled with the model's structure, has nonetheless proved consistently accurate. The raw estimates and the percentages are detailed in tables 4.1, 4.2, and 4.3.

International Context

Estimates of three separate sets of resources were collected, reflecting alternative timing and strategic options available to the British.

Scenario 1: Base case. This set of capability estimates reflected the aggregate pool of resources available to each group to influence the negotiations and, hence, their ultimate resolution. As illustrated in table 4.1, the strongest actor in the negotiations was the Chinese government, which controlled about 40 percent of the resources deemed applicable across the group of relevant actors. The second strongest actor was the Hong Kong local business community, with close to 29 percent of the total. The British government of Prime Minister Thatcher was third, controlling a scant 10 percent. This resource distribution underlies the belief that while Prime Minister Thatcher represented the negotiating arm of the British–Hong Kong coalition, the real force in that partnership resided in the enormous economic leverage of the local business community. By clustering the individuals in simple coalitions, the comparative shares appeared much less skewed, with Chinese interests controlling 50 percent, British/Hong Kong interests controlling 46 percent, and external actors holding the remaining 4 percent of resources.

Scenario 2: Decline in British resources over time. A second set of resource estimates was based on the assumption that, with

Table 4.1
International Context:
Groups and Their Overall Influence

Group	Scenario 1: Base Case		Scenario 2: British Decline		Scenario 3: British Gamble	
	level	%	level	%	level	%
Chinese Interests						
Chinese government	95.0	40	95.0	41	95.0	35
Chinese military	20.0	8	20.0	9	20.0	7
Guangdong faction	5.0	2	5.0	2	5.0	2
British Interests						
British government	23.0	10	20.7	9	53.0	20
Hong Kong Association	2.0	1	1.8	1	2.0	1
British traders	2.0	1	1.8	1	2.0	1
Hong Kong Interests						
Local business community	69.0	29	62.1	27	69.0	26
Foreign business community	7.0	3	7.0	3	7.0	3
Hong Kong Executive Council	7.0	3	6.3	3	7.0	3
International Observers						
International community	10.0	4	10.0	4	10.0	4

the passage of time, the capabilities of the British and the Hong Kong local business community would decline. This scenario assumed that, once an agreement was reached between the British/Hong Kong Executive Council and the Chinese, relative resource endowments would change in two ways. First, much of Britain's leverage would evaporate and, second, as time passes the economic community will vote with its feet, either by remaining in Hong Kong or by exporting capital and emigrating. Both alternatives reduce the future influence of the local business community. The impact of a prospective decline in influence was reflected in the analysis by a 10 percent reduction in the combined resources of the British, the Hong Kong Executive Council, and the Hong Kong local business community. This does not imply that the decline in influence of these groups will be limited to 10 percent. However, it illustrates how quickly the relationships between these groups and mainland China can change.

Scenario 3: British high-stakes gamble. There was widespread discussion of the possibility that the British could engage in a one-shot, high-stakes gamble on the future of Hong Kong. This strategy would have involved a British threat to oppose any unilateral Chinese action or to refuse to go along with an agreement that failed to include specific and explicit protections for the Hong Kong Chinese. We simulated these conditions by changing the resource endowments of the major players. Experts estimated how such a high-stakes gamble would affect Britain's net resources in the eyes of other players. The experts indicated that a high-risk strategy would have greatly increased the influence of the British, to a level approaching that of the Hong Kong local business community. This shift would have altered the balance of resources in favor of the combined British/Hong Kong interest, giving them control of 54 percent of total capabilities as opposed to 44 percent held by the Chinese coalition. The feasibility and anticipated outcome of such a strategy are analyzed in a later section.

Internal Hong Kong Context

For the internal Hong Kong analysis, only one aggregate measure of resources was provided—overall resources. As illustrated in table 4.2, the leftists (representing the interests of mainland China) are the strongest actor by far. They are rivaled by the combined influence of the Hong Kong business groups, though these groups do not alway adopt similar positions. The British influence, represented by the expatriate civil servants, is assumed to be 30 percent as strong as the leftists. The rest of the groups, though not very strong in their own right, may still play a critical role if they attach great salience to any particular issue.

Domestic Chinese Context

In the context of domestic Chinese policymaking on the future of Hong Kong, only one measure of resources, current

Table 4.2
Internal Hong Kong Context:
Groups and Their Overall Influence
(Base case)

	level	%
Political elite	20	6.8
Big local business	60	20.3
Small local business	10	3.4
British "Hongs"	10	3.4
Non-leftist workers	5	1.7
Expatriate civil servants	30	10.2
Middle-Level civil servants	20	6.8
Intellectuals	20	6.8
Leftists	100	33.9
International business	20	6.8

overall influence, was analyzed. As illustrated in table 4.3, the coalition of modernizers, Deng and the bureaucrats combined, are disproportionately influential. Only when these two groups separate on issues that they both care strongly about does a contest over outcomes become possible. Under such conditions the second tier of actors plays a pivotal role in determining the policy outcome.

THE IMPORTANCE OF THE ISSUES

Power alone does not guarantee success in political disputes. The will to win—embodied in our concept of salience—is critical in determining whether a group's power will be exercised in pursuit of the group's goals on a given issue. Tables 4.4, 4.5, and 4.6 depict the salience or importance each group attaches to each of the issues, first in the international context, then in the internal Hong Kong setting, and finally in terms of internal Chinese dynamics. Groups attaching low salience to an issue will commit few of their resources to influence a particular outcome, while groups exhibiting a high salience will exert a great deal of pressure to advance their cause.

Table 4.3
Domestic Chinese Context
Groups and Their Overall Influence
(Base case)

	level	%
Communist Party leadership	100	43
Bureaucracy	65	28
Communist Party ideologues	15	6
Modern military	25	11
Army	20	9
Guangdong Provincial leadership	10	4

ACTORS' POLICY PREFERENCES

The remaining data required by the expected utility model are the policy preferences of each actor on each of the issues that is considered. These preferences are displayed on issue continua that represent the plausible range of policy options. The end-points and some intermediate positions have been defined by leading experts, and each of the relevant actors has been placed on the continuum at the position it prefers. Groups may be omitted if they are truly indifferent among outcomes; thus all actors may not appear on all continua. For example, on the issue of the court system, the Chinese military is not represented because the experts indicated that this question does not impinge upon its interests in Hong Kong. All continua, along with the forecast for each issue, appear in chapters 5 and 6.

Table 4.4
International Context: Salience of Issues

Groups	Issues						
	Sovereignty	British Link	Free Market	Civil Rights	Courts	Currency	Leases
British government	0.7	1.0	1.0	1.0	1.0	1.0	1.0
Hong Kong Association	0.7	0.9	1.0	0.5	0.8	1.0	1.0
British traders	0.1	0.5	0.5	0.0	0.5	—	1.0
Chinese government	1.0	1.0	0.5	0.5	0.8	0.2	1.0
Chinese military	1.0	1.0	—	0.1	—	0.2	1.0
Guangdong faction	1.0	1.0	0.5	0.5	0.8	—	1.0
Hong Kong local business	0.7	1.0	1.0	0.8	1.0	1.0	1.0
Hong Kong foreign business	0.1	0.3	0.8	0.5	0.5	1.0	1.0
International observers	0.1	0.1	0.6	0.6	0.2	—	1.0
Hong Kong Executive Council	0.7	1.0	1.0	1.0	1.0	1.0	1.0

— Not Applicable

Table 4.5
Internal Hong Kong Context: Salience of Issues

Groups			Issues		
	Free market	Tax policy	Local representation	Labor regulation	Welfare spending
Political elite	0.8	0.8	1.0	0.3	1.0
Big local business	1.0	1.0	0.1	1.0	0.3
Small local business	1.0	1.0	—	—	—
British "Hongs"	1.0	1.0	0.1	1.0	0.3
Non-leftist workers	—	—	0.0	1.0	—
Expatriate civil servants	0.8	0.8	0.7	0.5	0.8
Mid-level civil servants	0.5	0.5	0.5	0.8	0.7
International business	1.0	1.0	0.1	1.0	0.3
Leftists	0.5	0.3	1.0	1.0	1.0
Intellectuals	0.2	0.3	1.0	1.0	1.0

— Not applicable

Table 4.6
Domestic Chinese Context: Salience of Issues

Groups	Issues				
	Free market	Civil liberties	Currency	Courts	Foreign Business restrictions
Deng Xiaoping	0.5	0.5	0.5	0.8	0.8
Bureaucracy	0.7	0.5	1.0	0.3	0.8
Communist Party ideologues	0.9	1.0	1.0	0.8	1.0
Modern military	—	0.1	0.2	0.1	0.5
Army	0.5	1.0	0.2	0.1	0.5
Guangdong faction	0.9	1.0	0.5	0.5	0.8

— Not Applicable

5
The International Negotiations

The British and Chinese share similar goals for Hong Kong's future. Both want to maintain the colony's political and economic health, recognizing that its economic prosperity stems from its autonomous and unrestricted economic development. They differ, however, over general assumptions and the specific policies necessary to guarantee Hong Kong's future vitality.

The major conclusions of this chapter can be highlighted briefly. Under the negotiated agreement between China and Britain, the British will not only surrender sovereignty, they will play *no* administrative role in Hong Kong after 1997. In the course of negotiation, the British sought to obtain explicit, formal guarantees intended to preserve the political and economic liberties that Hong Kong Chinese currently enjoy. The Chinese granted these guarantees, but, given the Chinese notion of sovereignty, the British have no way to prevent an erosion of these guarantees in the future. After 1997, China will try to maintain a "regulated" free market in Hong Kong somewhat akin to that which now exists in Taiwan, combining economic incentives with restrictions on political freedoms. China will permit full convertibility of the Hong Kong dollar, with assets externally held and autonomously controlled as a guarantee of the currency. But the courts, and with them all contracts, including property leases, will gradually come to resemble Chinese practice. The judicial system will drift slowly from the customs of Western commercial law in the direction of the legal conventions of the People's Republic of China. These are but a few of the highlights of our investigation. The remainder of this chapter presents a full analysis of the outcome of the Sino–British negotiations. Internal Hong Kong and domestic Chinese dynamics appear in chapter 6.

KEY CONCLUSIONS

Four key conclusions of our analysis of the future of Hong Kong emerged from the assumptions and data. We predicted:

1. *Sovereignty:* The settlement between Britain and China would transfer sovereignty over Hong Kong to China in 1997, with no administrative role for the British after 1997.
2. *Negotiation:* The constituencies of interests represented by the British and Chinese are extremely polarized, thus placing severe constraints on the range of feasible alternatives over which the negotiators could compromise.
3. *Stability:* The primary incentive of both main parties for reaching an agreement in 1984 was to preserve the political, economic, and social stability of Hong Kong through 1997.
4. *Impotence:* The British could do very little to impose their preferred solution.

Sovereignty

Would sovereign control over Hong Kong revert to China, or could it somehow be shared with Britain after 1997? This was one of the most critical issues facing the two parties. How this broad issue was resolved determined the policy stances of both sides on a number of concrete topics as well as determining the enforceability of any agreement.

The Chinese position on sovereignty is almost as old as the current treaties themselves: the return of sovereignty is non-negotiable. China views all three of the existing treaties as "unequal" and thus inapplicable to its political claim over the area. On this point, all groups with influence in the internal affairs of the People's Republic agree! But what do the Chinese mean by sovereignty? For them, sovereignty means that Chinese administration over the internal affairs of Hong Kong will not be subordinate to the will of any other state. Hence, legal sovereignty and administrative authority are inseparable. Against that viewpoint, China views any external enforcement mechanism as illegitimately interfering with its sovereign control. Britain's unconditional transfer renders mute any subsequent international enforcement of an agreement. The agreement rests solely on China's unilateral decision to honor it.

The British hoped that sovereignty might be shared. Titular sovereignty would revert to China, but Britain would maintain administrative responsibility in such areas as the police force, the currency, and the court system. All initial British proposals incorporated retention of British administrative responsibility after 1997, on the belief that a continued British presence was an essential condition for maintaining the economic health of the colony. Thus, a critical difference in the Chinese and British positions was the nature of the post-1997 Hong Kong link to Britain once sovereignty is transferred.

A possible Sino—British compromise involved an increase in local administrative autonomy. Day-to-day responsibility for Hong Kong affairs would devolve on the local inhabitants, who would control the local legislature, staff the police force, and operate the court system under Western commercial law. Presumably, these arrangements would preserve the future economic well-being of Hong Kong better than could direct control from Beijing. Localization, however, is not a full substitute for current British protection. After 1997, the guarantee of continued free exercise of local rule depends solely on China's good will. Local Hong Kong politicians will be ever fearful of the consequences of any decisions running contrary to the wishes of Beijing. Local control, then, can be quickly transformed into deference to Chinese wishes and, ultimately, direct Chinese control of Hong Kong.

In assessing the degree of control that might devolve to a

local Hong Kong administration, pessimism about the erosion of independence in Hong Kong must be tempered with the recognition of how much the Chinese stand to lose by depriving the territory of its autonomy. China receives 30 to 40 percent of its foreign exchange earnings through Hong Kong. As of 1984, China holds some US$3 to $4 billion of direct investment in Hong Kong and may soon surpass the United States as Hong Kong's largest foreign investor. The value and future yield of these assets would be jeopardized by an international loss of confidence in the Hong Kong economy. The risks are well recognized within China and represent a central point of contention among Chinese ruling elites.

Our analysis of internal Chinese policy shows, for instance, that the modernizers and the ideological old guard are engaged in an intense battle over whether maintaining Hong Kong's capitalist economy is consistent with China's goals. The key figure among the modernizers is Deng Xiaoping, who is pressing for an early settlement in order to leverage his influence and exploit pressures from the international community to his advantage.

These three options—a transfer of sovereignty, shared sovereignty, or localization of authority—defined the context of any settlement. The only option that would have guaranteed the preservation of the status quo was shared sovereignty, with the British retaining administrative control over the police, courts, and financial secretariat. A post-1997 British presence would have precluded direct Chinese management of key administrative functions. The settlement, which incorporates a transfer of legal sovereignty from Britain to China, although it provides for increased local control, throws into question the guarantees of economic and political rights, especially since the next generation of Chinese leaders may be less committed to modernization than Deng Xiaoping. Our forecast of a transfer of sovereignty implied that, unless external pressures compel them to do so, China cannot be counted on to honor its promise not to intervene later in Hong Kong affairs. At present, under almost all conceivable scenarios, the prospects for such external pressure are extremely remote.

The Negotiating Context

The negotiations, though nominally involving only the British and Chinese governments, entailed complex interactions among diverse interests within China, Hong Kong, Britain, and the international community. China's negotiating team had to take into account disputes among the different Chinese elites on such matters as limitations on free trade and autonomy for Hong Kong's judicial system. At the same time, they had to be mindful of pressures from Britain and other foreign communities. China's elites, including its bureaucratic leadership, military officials, and keepers of the party line, can impose heavy political costs on the current leadership should Deng Xiaoping, Hu Yaobang, and Zhao Ziyang wholly disregard their demands. On the other hand, Deng and his associates cannot ignore the hard reality that local Hong Kong and foreign interests control the bulk of the financial resources of Hong Kong. If Deng had bent too far in accommodating his domestic constituency, he could have faced intransigence from British and Hong Kong interests at the negotiating table. Such intransigence, coupled with failure to reach a negotiated settlement, would have represented a high international cost for Deng; loss of access to foreign capital, technology, and trade could severely damage his ambitions to modernize China.

From the perspective of key conservative groups in China, Deng appeared too accommodating to the British, who signify the one remaining open sore of China's historical disgrace. On preserving Western-style civil liberties, maintaining a judicial system independent of Chinese jurisdiction, and retaining capitalism, Deng was seen by his colleagues as a right-wing extremist, often standing alone in his support for a "pro-British" position. Yet, from Britain's point of view, China seemed intransigent, inflexible, and unwilling to compromise. The British, no doubt, perceived themselves as quite moderate, having in many cases adopted policies more amenable to the Chinese perspective than had many of the indigenous Hong Kong interests. But Britain's "accommodation" of Chinese concerns appeared minimal to Deng and his supporters.

The simplified issue continuum below graphically displays this Sino—British polarization and the contentiousness it engenders (figure 5.1). In those situations where Deng adopted a position that was more conciliatory or "pro-British" than other key Chinese actors, domestic political pressures made it almost impossible for him to moderate his policies. The British, who in many instances were in a more flexible position than indigenous Hong Kong interests, were similarly constrained from further compromise.

Deng's need to respond to domestic Chinese pressures coupled with Britain's need to accommodate Hong Kong interests opened an almost unbridgeable gap between the two parties. Deng did not believe he could move much more toward the British and still manage his internal political affairs. The British saw no advantage in moving much closer to Deng's demands unless such movement was matched by compromise from the Chinese. If the British believed Deng had gone as far as he would go in guaranteeing Hong Kong's future, then their incentive was to wait until external financial and political pressure forced him to move more—although they did not want to run the risk of having to deal with the next generation of Chinese leaders. Deng's successors are likely to be even more constrained by domestic considerations. This fear of future risks drove the British to acquiesce to most Chinese demands even when concessions could have been obtained. The British perceived the price of even partial success as too high to warrant the risks of failure.

Figure 5.1
China and Britain: Simplified Position Continuum

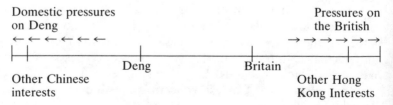

Stability

The taxicab strike, minor street riots, increased crime, as well as the roller-coaster ride of the economy since the September 1982 announcement all indicate the potential for disruption that Hong Kong faces during the thirteen transitional years to 1997. Since China will unconditionally recover sovereignty and the British will have little influence over the maintenance or implementation of the accord, one purpose of the negotiations was to ease the transition with minimal social and economic disruption.

Britain's sole trump card was China's concern that the absence of a mutually agreed settlement might seriously erode Hong Kong's economy, and thus its benefit to China's development plans. On this strength, Prime Minister Thatcher had three options. She reached an acceptable agreement by China's stated deadline of September 1984. She could have followed a risky course by issuing a "take it or leave it" ultimatum. Or she could have stalled, using the continuing flight of capital and skilled labor as leverage to force concessions. Uncertainty threatens stability. Our expected utility analysis indicates that such a delay tactic would have represented Britain's best approach, although they still would not have gained much.

Impotence

Regardless of the course Britain pursued, it was in a weak position to impose its preferred policies. Britain held little leverage over China except on such issues as an independent, convertible currency and maintaining current land lease arrangements. Even a high risk "take it or leave it" strategy held little hope of wringing major substantive concessions from China.

If Britain had adopted a delay strategy and insisted that a formal agreement to transfer sovereignty be linked to some administrative concessions, it could have obtained some small gains. However, the delaying strategy could not have been very long-lived. The erosion of Britain's relations with China and the flight of capital that would have been associated with this strategy would have ultimately left Britain in a very risky situation should China have broken off the talks. While such a response would also have been very costly to Deng Xiaoping, important elements in the Chinese military and in the Communist party would have supported such a step before endorsing any linkage.

THE SETTLEMENT

As previously stated, the future prosperity and political freedoms of Hong Kong revolve around the conditions imposed on the transfer of sovereignty. China's position is that sovereignty is not negotiable. Despite disagreements among key groups on other policy questions within China, unanimity reigns on this point: sovereignty must be unconditionally returned to China. The British are willing, and indeed have no choice, to concede titular sovereignty, but they sought in exchange guarantees that China will preserve the current commercial structures and political freedoms of the people of Hong Kong. Our analysis indicated that the Chinese would provide some, but not all, of the guarantees sought by the British.

The reason for China's willingness to compromise is straightforward. The Chinese definition of sovereignty precluded any binding constraints on the policies they adopt after 1997. By granting guarantees now, the Chinese may forestall a financial panic in Hong Kong. Later, if the modernizers continue to dominate Chinese politics, only a modest reduction of the guarantees is anticipated. If, however, China swings in the other direction, the more ideological elements may abrogate any guarantees that the current regime offers.

However generous current Chinese compromises may appear, guarantees of Hong Kong's future will gradually dissipate. To see how and why, consider the example of the continuation of the territory's free market economy. The Hong Kong business community, the Hong Kong Executive Council, and the Hong Kong Association all support such a continuation. The British government, British traders, foreign business interests, and the international community are willing to tolerate some limits on economic freedom and would accept a somewhat more regulated system resembling that of Taiwan. Deng favors retaining free market forces, though he advocates more restrictions than now exist in Taiwan; on the other hand, the civil bureaucracy, the army, and the Party ideologues within China all support a fully controlled, socialist economy. Obviously, there is considerable difference of opinion on how best to treat Hong Kong's economy.

If the issue were resolved solely in the context of the 1984 negotiations, we forecast that the British preference for a Taiwan-style economy would prevail in Hong Kong after 1997. Such a policy represents a tolerable compromise to Deng Xiaoping in the context of the international pressures he faces. Indeed, such a guarantee is exactly the sort of policy that is likely to help reassure nervous investors that Hong Kong will remain safe. Yet, as the years unfold, Deng's supporters among the modernization group (including the air force, navy, missile brigades, and such important civilian leaders as Hu Yaobang) will have to come to terms with the reality that this compromise is not acceptable to most of the Chinese elite. In fact, as the issue becomes internalized in the Chinese political process, we forecast that the reinterpreted policy of the People's Republic of China toward Hong Kong will be only slightly more liberal than their internal economic policy in 1997.

STRATEGIC OPTIONS OPEN TO BRITAIN

The British were criticized, especially by some in Hong Kong, for opening the negotiations so far in advance of the expiration of the lease. The results of our analysis indicate, however, that this strategy was sensible, given Britain's declining ability to influence the settlement. Our methodology permitted us to examine rigorously the question of timing: Which side would benefit from the passage of time? How would changes in political and economic leverage influence the ultimate implementation of the settlement?

Hong Kong experts indicate that the influence of the British and indigenous Hong Kong actors was at its peak as the negotiations opened. The passage of time diminishes the resources and influence of these groups relative to those of China. The leverage of the Hong Kong community declines with the outflow of each dollar and the emigration of each entrepreneur and skilled professional. The British lost resources and influence the moment they announced an agreement with the Chinese, because they could no longer threaten to break off the talks. Now that the agreement is signed, Britain's charge that China is not living up to its promises is likely to lack credibility and to suggest only that Britain should never have signed an accord in the first place. Accordingly, Britain's role during the next thirteen years will decline. The sharpest fall came when they publicly acknowledged an agreement. On the other hand, our analysis indicated that the appearance of intransigence on the part of the British would have improved their ability to extract some additional concessions from China. It thus seemed in the interest of Britain and Hong Kong to reach a settlement in the medium term, over a few years, but not necessarily within a matter of months.

The analysis shows that China stood to gain more by an earlier settlement or by a much later settlement. That, presumably, is why Deng Xiaoping imposed a September deadline. He knew the medium term favored Britain, and he did not wish to incur the substantial costs of waiting for the long term (1990 or beyond), by which time severe financial stress would likely have settled upon Hong Kong.

Observers of Hong Kong have tried to analyze the likelihood and the effect of the British adopting a high-risk, "take it or leave it" attitude toward the Chinese. In assuming such a stance, the British would have indicated that an acceptable settlement had to contain an irreducible core of provisions that explicitly insured the future political and economic health of the colony. Failing these provisions, Britain would have refused to turn Hong Kong over to China, though they could not obstruct China from occupying the territory and taking control. Furthermore, Britain could have warned China that it would not try to protect such Chinese interests as preserving Hong Kong quotas under the Multi-Fibre Arrangement.

In order to investigate the feasibility of such a strategy in 1984, we used the model to simulate the impact of a British ultimatum to the Chinese (using the distribution of resources set forth in scenario 3 of chapter 4). We then examined what policy shifts would result from a short but dramatic economic downturn brought on by a high-risk British strategy. The analysis indicates that a high-risk policy would increase the contentiousness of many of the issues, but would have little impact on the actual policies that would be adopted. Britain could have precipitated a political crisis through the issuance of an ultimatum, but such a strategy was not likely to change significantly any of the policy outcomes. Consequently, an ultimatum would not have served Britain's interests.

WHY SETTLE IN 1984?

The central motivation for reaching an agreement in 1984 was to preserve civil order and financial stability in Hong Kong as far into the next decade as possible. We assumed that neither Britain nor China wanted responsibility for a breakdown in civil order. Despite public statements from China that they would intervene in the case of disorder, our analysis indicated that this threat was only posturing. If the agreement preserves civil order and permits a limited but orderly exit of capital and people through 1997, then it will have served one of its most important functions.

What else will the agreement do? As we have indicted, an agreement which transfers sovereignty lacks any mechanism for future enforcement of specific provisions and guarantees. Consequently, the agreement constrained the spectrum over which political groups compete; policies on critical issues were limited to a narrower set of feasible alternatives. On the issue of civil liberties, for instance, full protection of civil rights was no longer an option. Rather, the contest was over how far civil liberties will be allowed to erode. The agreement constrained and redefined the political debate by removing many of the liberal alternatives.

For Deng, it was very important to reach a settlement in 1984. As noted, he faced considerable opposition within China to his liberal policies toward Hong Kong. The presence of international pressure to concede economic and political guarantees provided Deng with a politically viable justification for granting concessions and, thereby, helped him protect his modernization program in China. The longer it took to reach a settlement, the more people were likely to shift financial resources out of Hong Kong, and the less Hong Kong could be counted on to provide financial assistance for economic growth in the People's Republic.

Given China's pressure for a settlement in 1984 and Britain's mixed motivations to sign or delay, we expected that progress toward a settlement would occur in 1984. It did not appear, however, that there was sufficient time or motivation on the part of the British to reach a full accord, in which every *i* is dotted and every *t* crossed, by the end of the year. Rather, we expected to see the general principles of an agreement worked out, but some important details and provisions concerning implementation remaining unresolved. Indeed, the joint declaration is vague. The Chinese have not yet unveiled their specific plans for Hong Kong's governance, although they have promised to produce Hong Kong's Basic Law(i.e., constitution) by 1990. The Chinese government agreed to consult with local Hong Kong leaders in preparing the Basic Law, but they are not bound to accept the advice they receive. In fact, China did not even agree to specify in advance the mechanism by which the Hong Kong chief executive will be selected. This is as if the American colonies in 1787 had ratified a constitution calling for a president, but failed to agree on how the president would be selected. China has made no binding concessions regarding the details of Hong Kong's future political structure.

The rest of this chapter presents an issue-by-issue summary of our analysis, including sovereignty and linkage, the free marketplace, civil freedoms, courts, currency, and leases and rents. These concrete issues plus the major points of negotiation discussed in this chapter cover much of the policy agenda that will be affected by a change in Hong Kong's status. This list of issues also reflects the major concerns of the international community.

This chapter addresses not only the specific outcome we forecast for each issue, but also the attributes of the negotiating parties and their strategies, which are critical in determining the expected policy change. Thus, without burdening the reader with too much political analysis, we nevertheless want to reveal some of the logic upon which the results are based.

We present each issue in a consistent format to reflect the information gathered from experts (used as inputs to the model), along with the forecast derived from the model. For each issue, we draw a graphic display of the issue spectrum and label the anticipated policy outcomes. The graphs depict the policy preferences of all the groups relevant to that issue, as well as the point forecast derived from the expected utility model. (Recall from chapter 2 that the model also requires data on relative group resources and the salience of an issue for each group, and that the model estimates each group's willingness to take risks.)

We also examine the context of the forecasted policy decision. For each issue we provide a summary of the analysis that led to the policy forecast. These discussions and the accompanying Cartesian diagrams outline the relationships between the various groups. It is precisely these dynamics that underlie the specific policy forecasts. All policy inferences are drawn exclusively from the logic of the model, coupled with the input information provided by experts. Expert judgments are not used to reach conclusions about policy decisions or to draw inferences about the political contentiousness of particular issues.

A careful analysis of these political dynamics provides essential information on how each issue is resolved. For instance, a contentious issue, one on which groups believe that they can impose a settlement favoring their position, is more difficult to resolve than an issue on which the parties believe that they need to compromise. Take, for example, the issue of how extensive a free market Hong Kong should have. Both the Chinese and the Hong Kong business interests believe that they can force the other side to make concessions. This is the sort of policy dispute that is not easily resolved. Conversely, the issue of travel restrictions is not contentious and thus is easily resolved.

It is important to bear in mind this distinction between contentious and noncontentious issues, for it has serious implications in an evaluation of the Hong Kong settlement. An agreement that addressed only those issues identified as less contentious, leaving the specifics of the contentious issues for a later date, would have simply postponed the fight between the Chinese and the Hong Kong interests. On the other hand, a settlement that specifically addresses the contentious issues provides a strong foundation for a negotiated transfer. This section addresses the following questions:

1. Which actors influence the outcome of this issue and what positions do they hold?
2. Is the issue likely to be settled in an environment of contentiousness? Do many groups believe they can impose their preferred outcome (i.e., do they fall in octants 1 and 2 of the Cartesian diagrams)? Or is an easy compromise anticipated (where the winners and losers clearly know who they are)?
3. Which groups are most likely to win or lose on the issue? Do they correctly perceive their ability to influence the outcome, or are they likely to make strategic mistakes that could be costly in terms of their ability to influence this or other issue outcomes?
4. Can the forecast outcome be changed by employing alternative negotiating strategies, such as delays or "take it or leave it" tactics?
5. Is the forecast outcome a stable one, or will the policy erode over time due to changing conditions or relative influence among groups?

All of the analyses presented in this section are derived directly from the model.

SOVEREIGNTY AND AN ADMINISTRATIVE LINK WITH BRITAIN

Issue. Where will sovereignty reside and will the British maintain an administrative link with Hong Kong?
Forecast. The Sino–British negotiations will provide for a transfer of sovereignty from the British to the Chinese. In addition, the British will not be able to extract any formal concessions that provide for a British administrative role after 1997.

On the issue of sovereignty, all of the internal Chinese groups and international actors preferred a policy that provides for a complete transfer. The British, the Executive Council, and the Hong Kong business community all were willing to accept a transfer as long as it was accompanied with assurances that cannot be unilaterally rejected by the Chinese some time in the future. Only the Hong Kong Association sought a special role for the British in post-1997 Hong Kong.

Figure 5.2
Forecast: Sovereignty and Administrative Link

ISSUE: What policy will be adopted on the transfer of sovereignty over Hong Kong and Kowloon?

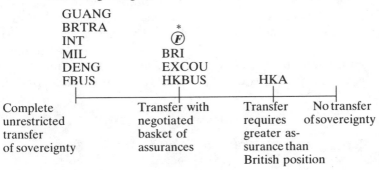

```
        GUANG
        BRTRA          *
        INT           Ⓕ
        MIL           BRI
        DENG          EXCOU
        FBUS          HKBUS         HKA
        ├─────────────┼─────────────┼─────────────┤
Complete      Transfer with      Transfer      No transfer
unrestricted  negotiated         requires      of sovereignty
transfer      basket of          greater as-
of sovereignty assurances        surance than
                                  British position
```

* Actual outcome. See the joint declaration and annexes
Ⓕ Forecast outcome.

ISSUE: What policy will be adopted on a link between Britain and Hong Kong?

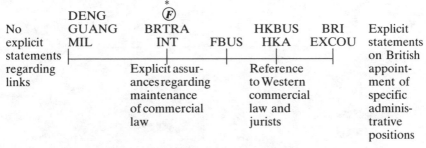

```
              DENG        *
No            GUANG      Ⓕ
explicit      MIL        BRTRA                HKBUS      BRI     Explicit
statements    ├──────────┼─────────┼─────────┼──────────┤       statements
regarding                INT      FBUS       HKA        EXCOU   on British
links                    Explicit assur-     Reference          appoint-
                         ances regarding     to Western         ment of
                         maintenance         commercial         specific
                         of commercial       law and            adminis-
                         law                 jurists            trative
                                                                positions
```

Groups: BRI = British government
      BRTRA = British traders
       DENG = Chinese government
     EXCOU = Hong Kong Executive Council
       FBUS = Hong Kong foreign business
    GUANG = Guangdong faction
        HKA = Hong Kong Association
    HKBUS = Hong Kong local business
         INT = International community
        MIL = Chinese military

* Actual outcome. See the joint declaration and annexes.

As noted earlier, the forecast resolution of this issue was for a complete transfer of sovereignty, accompanied by some Chinese assurances to maintain Hong Kong's freedoms, but not enough to satisfy Britain. The analysis indicates that the Hong Kong interests did not perceive much opportunity to alter the position taken by Deng. However, as seen in figures 5.3 and 5.4, Deng, the British, the Hongs, and local businesses perceived that the Hong Kong groups would be able to extract some compromise from the hard-line position advanced by the Chinese government. The extent of this leverage, however, was not suffi-

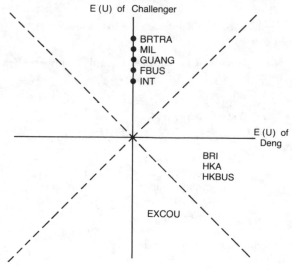

Figure 5.3

Sovereignty: Challenger's Perspective

Groups:

BRI	British government	GUANG	Guangdong faction
BRTRA	British traders	HKA	Hong Kong Association
DENG	Chinese government	HKBUS	Hong Kong local business community
EXCOU	Hong Kong Executive Council	INT	The United States and other countries
FBUS	Hong Kong foreign business community	MIL	Chinese military

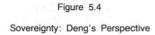

Figure 5.4

Sovereignty: Deng's Perspective

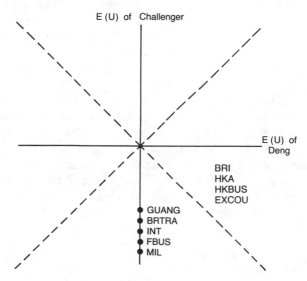

E (U) of Challenger

E (U) of Deng

BRI
HKA
HKBUS
EXCOU

● GUANG
● BRTRA
● INT
● FBUS
● MIL

cient to produce enforceable assurances, but only formalistic promises.

Failing the retention of sovereignty, the second most important British objective was to retain a formal administrative link with Hong Kong after 1997. On this matter, the range of preferences was much broader. On one end were the internal Chinese groups (Deng, the Guangdong faction, and the military) who preferred that no explicit statements regarding a link be incorporated into the settlement. International actors and the various non–Hong Kong business interests all preferred that the British role be sufficient to assure their continued commercial operations. Finally, Hong Kong business and the Hongs preferred even greater assurances of the legal system, while the British and the Hong Kong Executive Council pressed for a formal administrative role that would allow the British to appoint officials to specific positions such as the courts and police.

Our analysis indicated that the resolution of this issue would provide for explicit assurances regarding commercial law. It predicted that negotiations over this issue would be heated between Deng and the Hong Kong business interests, as each believed that it has the upper hand on the issue (figures 5.5, 5.6). The British, the British traders and the international business interests perceived that they could partially overcome Deng's preferences, although they recognized that the outcome will favor the Chinese view more than their own. Deng, for his part, was willing to accept some compromise, although he believed the real pressure came from the British and the key Hong Kong interests, not from the international community. In the final resolution of this issue, the combined leverage of the various Hong Kong–British pressure groups produced the compromise outcome that provides explicit assurances but not iron-clad guarantees, as noted above.

Figure 5.5

Britain-Hong Kong Link: Challenger's Perspective

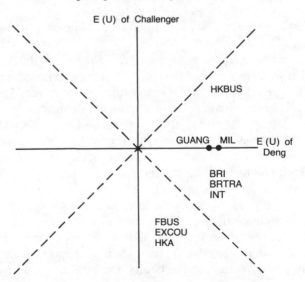

Figure 5.6

Britain-Hong Kong Link: Deng's Perspective

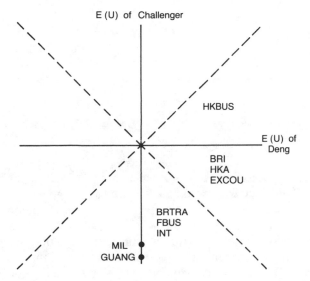

FREE MARKET

Issue. How open a marketplace will Hong Kong be?
Forecast. The Sino–British negotiations will result in a modest erosion of the free market as it currently exists in Hong Kong. Economic restrictions and government constraints will gradually produce an economic system resembling that found in Taiwan or Malaysia.

The issue of how much regulation will be imposed on the colony's free market economy was central to the fabric of the settlements. Mainland Chinese groups held the position that a capitalistic system can be abusive and counterproductive; they preferred policies that would end speculation in land, stocks, and currency. The Hong Kong Association, the local businesses, and the Executive Council all demanded the maintenance of the status quo, an open and unregulated marketplace. Britain, along with the international business and political community was willing to accept some additional controls that might transform

Figure 5.7
Forecast: Free Market

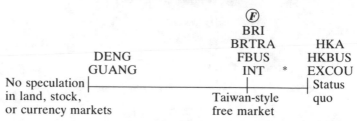

* Actual outcome. See the joint declaration, paragraph 3, subparagraphs 5-10 and 12.

the territory's economy to resemble Taiwan or Malaysia. These controls could involve an increased role for the government in economic planning and in setting priorities for development and the coordination of investment.

Our analysis of this critical question indicated that the issue would be highly contentious. As a consequence of the political discord, this issue was difficult to resolve and could well have extended the length of time needed to reach an accord. The ultimate settlement revolved around a contest between the Hong Kong business interests and the Chinese, in which the Hong Kong business group held a more advantageous position.

What made this issue so difficult was each side's belief that it had an opportunity to achieve all of its policy demands without having to compromise. Deng viewed his relationships with Hong Kong business, the Executive Council, and the Hongs as difficult (note these groups fall in octants 1 and 2 of figure 5.8), but still he saw himself as winning in the end. These groups, as well as the British, British traders, foreign business, and international interests, in turn, all believed that they could defeat China's position (see figure 5.9). However, all of these groups, with the exception of local business, believed that Deng has some advantage in any conflict. Ultimately, the Hong Kong business community and their supporters were able to extract the major concession outlined in our forecast, largely defeating the Chinese government on this issue.

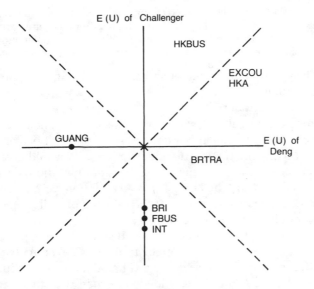

Figure 5.8

Free Market: Deng's Perspective

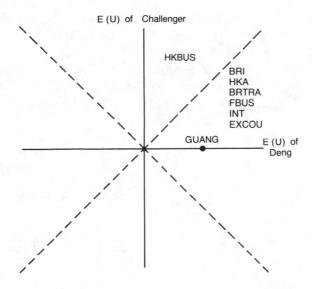

Figure 5.9

Free Market: Challenger's Perspective

CIVIL LIBERTIES

Issue. What policy will be adopted toward civil liberties in Hong Kong?
Forecast. The international settlement will pave the way for an erosion
of civil liberties in Hong Kong including prohibitions on open criticism
of the Chinese government and on public political demonstrations.

The British and Hong Kong Executive Council supported
the maintenance of current civil liberties. The Chinese groups
and the British traders all favored the civil rights incorporated in
the Chinese constitution (which can be suspended under Article
51 when the government's interests so dictate). Local Hong
Kong business and the international community would accept a
slight erosion of the status quo as a compromise solution. Finally,
foreign business and the Hong Kong Association were willing to
preserve commercial freedoms at the expense of civil freedoms.
It was very important to the British and business community of
Hong Kong that this issue be addressed squarely by the accord,
because they recognized that on the transfer of sovereignty their
influence over the policies adopted will be significantly reduced.
Conversely, the Chinese were less concerned with the specific
content of the accords because many of the policies ultimately
adopted will be resolved within the domestic Chinese political
environment.

This issue was controversial. Almost all of the groups expected their policy preferences to prevail, making an amicably

Figure 5.10
Forecast: Civil Liberties

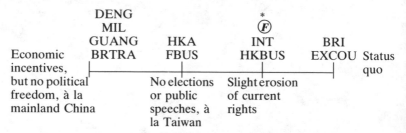

* Actual outcome. See annex I, section XIII and the memorandum of the United
Kingdom.

negotiated resolution difficult. (From everyone's perspective, the political dynamics surrounding civil liberties propelled conflicts of the sort that arise when groups are in octants 1 and 2 of our Cartesian diagrams.) The central contest was between Deng and the Hong Kong business community. The forecast settlement was the product of policy compromises that arose from the high cost to Deng for continuing to insist on his most preferred position. The other side also had to pay a heavy price, which their salience scores indicated they were more prepared to do than was the Chinese government. They cared more, so they were willing to spend more.

A high-risk "take it or leave it" strategy on the part of Britain would have produced more guarantees, thus better insuring the maintenance of the status quo. Under such a strategy, the issue would have remained contentious between Deng and the business interests, but Deng's ability to alter the outcome would have been slightly diminished.

COURTS

Issue: What policy will be adopted toward the court system?
Forecast: The Sino−British agreement will allow the court of final authority to be independent, with local judges operating under Western law.

Figure 5.11
Forecast: Courts

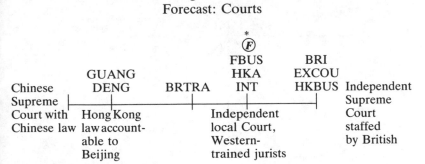

* Actual outcome. See annex I, section III.

The range of alternatives on this issue was bound by a British-controlled court system on the one had and a system of courts subject to Beijing's control on the other. The Chinese favored an arrangement whereby the courts would operate under Hong Kong law, not China's, but would be accountable to Beijing. The position favored by the British, the Executive Council, and local business called for an independent Hong Kong court staffed by British judges. International business and the international community preferred the maintenance of independent courts with local judges operating under Western law. British traders operating in China, not needing the same protections as those with plant and personnel in Hong Kong, were indifferent between the Chinese and international business position.

Our analysis indicated that the central contest on this issue

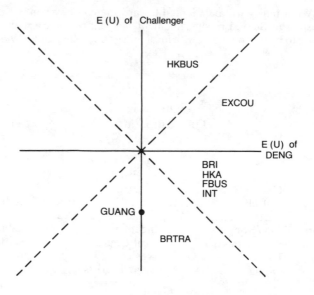

Figure 5.12

Courts: Deng's Perspective

Figure 5.13

Courts: Challenger's Perspective

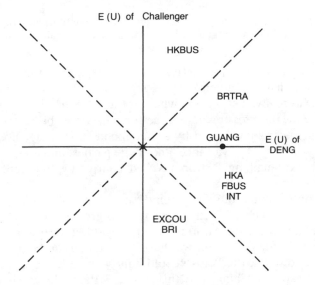

was again between Deng and the local business interests (figures 5.12 and 5.13). Both sides perceived the issue to be conflictual, with local business interests in the strongest position (this group falls in octant 2 from both Deng's and the challenger's perspectives). The highly contentious nature of the debate made intransigence very costly, prompting the modest compromise outlined in figure 5.11. As is evident from figure 5.12, Deng recognized the need to compromise with the groups that occupied our forecast position. Neither a high-risk strategy nor a delay strategy by the British would have improved the outcome for the Hong Kong interests. The agreement reached in September 1984 is precisely the same as our forecast. The danger for the future lies in the absence of any mechanism that would prevent political pressures from Beijing from influencing judicial proceedings in Hong Kong.

CURRENCY

Issue: What policy will be adopted toward the Hong Kong currency and its international convertibility?
Forecast: The accord will provide for the establishment of an independent currency board charged with controlling and maintaining a separate, convertible Hong Kong currency.

The parties did not disagree over a separate Hong Kong currency; an independent Hong Kong dollar will be maintained. What was really at stake was whether the Bank of China would manage the reserves or whether the currency would be backed by external asserts controlled by an independent currency board. There was very little variance among the parties, and only Deng and the Guangdong faction favored control by the Bank of China.

Consequently, our analysis indicated that this issue was one of the few in which the British – Hong Kong groups would achieve their exact objective. Although the policy differences appeared to be small, the resolution would be disputatious and not easily settled; however, the British could impose an independent currency board on China. On this issue, Britain's leverage was

Figure 5.14
Forecast: Currency

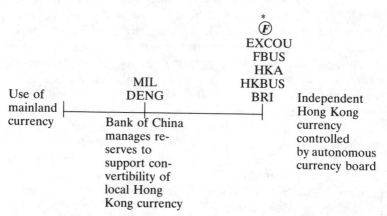

* Actual outcome. See annex I, section VII.

considerable, due both to the influence wielded by its coalition partners and to the fact that Britain controlled the Hong Kong Exchange Fund at the time and could not be forced to return these reserves.

This issue was also significant because it provided the British with the opportunity to institutionalize a credible guarantee concerning Hong Kong's future. If the currency board is properly structured and truly independent, it is unlikely that domestic Chinese politics can erode it. The only alternative available to the Chinese would have been to opt for the costly step of eliminating the Hong Kong currency and losing the reserves. In the end, China agreed to allow the Hong Kong dollar to remain freely convertible and fully backed by externally held assets.

LEASES AND PROPERTY RIGHTS

Issue: What policy will be adopted in regard to property, assuming Crown titles transfer to China?
Forecast: All of the land currently under Crown title will be transferred to the Chinese with the change of sovereignty. The policy adopted will be for a maintenance of current leases and a renewal at market rates when they expire.

Figure 5.15
Forecast: Leases and Property Rights

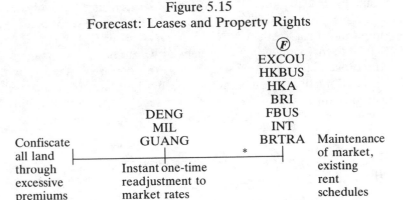

* Actual outcome. See annex III.

Currently all land in Hong Kong is owned by the Crown and is made available for private use under long-term leases. Leases in Hong Kong and Kowloon extend beyond 1997 since the treaties covering this area were not, in the British view, subject to expiration. Leases in the New Territories were all written to expire in 1997.

The possible alternatives on this issue ranged from complete nationalization of land by the Chinese to an honoring of all current leases, with good-faith negotiations based on market rates when they expire. The Chinese position on the leases supported a one-time readjustment to market rates and then adherence to those rates reflecting real changes in annual values, whereas the British–Hong Kong interests favored honoring of all leases and a good-faith renewal of leases as they come to term. Legally, the difference in lease rates on July 1, 1997 only affects Kowloon and Hong Kong Island as all leases in the New Territories expire in 1997 and thus would require renegotiation even if Britain were to retain sovereignty. British policy is to renew at market rates for a fixed term, but to retain the annual nominal rental over the duration of the term. Therefore, if land values rise, the Chinese policy imposes higher costs on landholders than does the British.

Deng was prepared to accept a compromise favorable to the British point of view. For the British, accepting China's position could have been politically costly, as local interests were likely to view such a concession as a sellout. This was an exceptionally important issue (salience = 1.0 for every group).

Alternative negotiating strategies would not have changed the outcome. In some cases, such as the high-risk "take it or leave it" tactic, the outcome produced might have been a one-shot readjustment of rents to market levels. This result would have been less favorable to the British than the compromise we forecast.

COMPARISON OF THE FORECASTS WITH THE JOINT DECLARATION

On all issues except that pertaining to property leases, the expected utility forecasts of March 1984 mirror the contents of the joint declaration that the governments of China and Britain initialled on September 26, 1984. The divergence between the forecast and the terms of the agreement on leases is very modest indeed, consisting only of the difference between the cash value of annually adjustable rates and fixed nominal rate for a specific rental term. Our error arose because a key alternative was not identified in the issue continuum. We forecast a compromise. The experts did not anticipate that the Chinese would also press a claim for a portion of all land sales between now and 1997, while also restricting the quantity of annual land sales.

Because the British, as forecast, unconditionally transferred sovereignty and dissolved the British link (in exchange for unenforceable written assurances), the remaining issues should be seen as minor skirmishes by comparison. The field of battle needed to be over control of Hong Kong. According to our analysis, the British could not succeed on these questions (although our simulations of alternative strategies showed that small concessions even on these issues could have been extracted if the British had pursued a delaying tactic). Because they did not utilize a delay strategy, they had no way to win on the two fundamental questions. The British could only hope to extract such relatively small concessions here and there as we forecast on the other lesser issues. And this they did except in the case of property leases.

6
The Post-Agreement Administration of Hong Kong

From the day the British Parliament ratified the Sino—British accord on Hong Kong, thereby revoking the 1842 and 1860 treaties, until the stroke of midnight on June 30, 1997, when sovereignty reverts to China, Hong Kong is in a twelve-year transition period. Life will go on in the twilight years of British colonial administration, but the colony's political culture will undergo a transformation from acceptance of colonial rule to maneuvering by different groups seeking to enhance their political standing and implement their policies during the transition years. What will happen in that narrow space of time? How will Hong Kong's political, economic, and social fabric change? What can be gleaned about the more distant future from forecasts of policy shifts within Hong Kong and the People's Republic of China during the sunset years of Britain's sole remaining major colony?

China has repeatedly expressed its intention to maintain Hong Kong's special character, which is borne out in the expected utility analyses of the international negotiations. The model forecasts that China will maintain the territory's free market economy, current civil liberties, and British commercial law. Conceivably, the Sino—British accord could restore confidence in Hong Kong's future under Chinese administration. In fact, the stock market put on a sustained rally during the second half of 1984 that has continued in early 1985 now that the terms of the Joint Declaration are clear. After all, China's resumption of sovereignty does not rule out its written commitment to allow Hong Kong people to maintain their own social, economic, and legal systems separate from those in China.

But would confidence be warranted? However well intentioned Deng Xiaoping may be, can Hong Kong's more than five million residents count on the Chinese to honor their promises? Will the signing of an agreement unleash political forces within Hong Kong that will press for serious changes in economic, social, and political policies during the crucial transition years? How will the governance of Hong Kong change during these remaining twelve years of British control? Will Hong Kong retain civil liberties, low taxes, and free movement of capital and labor, or will the transition years see movement away from a laissez-faire society toward a Western-style, welfare-state democracy? Will China encourage a system of governance in Hong Kong that preserves a capitalist, speculative marketplace in the midst of a communist regime that has thus far tolerated few civil or economic freedoms?

The years 1985 to 1997 place Hong Kong in a sort of limbo. Though Hong Kong is legally still controlled and administered by Britain, China's influence over the politics and even the daily affairs of Hong Kong will steadily grow. Two factors will determine the focus of policy discussions during this twelve-year transition. One is to anticipate what the Chinese will want to do after 1997. The other is to try to place limits on what the Chinese can do. The British administration will become a lame duck. As 1997 draws near, few if any incentives will exist for political actors to pursue a course of action whose primary purpose is to curry favor or political advantage from the British.

Although China's interests will officially be on Hong Kong's back burner for the immediate years, they will be very much the center of attention and maneuvering. British measures to alter the form of government in Hong Kong will reflect their desire to constrain subsequent policy options available to China. Efforts will be made to institutionalize a system of independent, local administration. That administration will encourage local elites to form political parties and seek popular support and financial backing. In short, the British will try to construct for Hong Kong an independent political system that can resist Chinese influence. They will try to constrain China's political options by insuring that these institutions are so well engrained in Hong Kong's political life that their abandonment would embarrass China and endanger its aspirations for economic modernization, international legitimation, and especially the recovery of Taiwan along lines similar to those worked out for Hong Kong.

Both Britain and China support the development of more representative government, though not necessarily leading to a one man, one vote parliamentary democracy. The British presume that local representative institutions will constrain subsequent policy options available to China. The leadership in Beijing may see the expansion of representative government in Hong Kong as an opportunity to influence policy during the transition, especially in increasing modestly the regulation of markets and labor conditions. On these issues, China wants to gain support without jeopardizing Hong Kong's economic value. China would prefer inheriting a financially viable Hong Kong even at the expense of sacrificing opportunities to buy popular favor through a broad expansion of social programs. The local political activists among intellectuals would like to build a democratic welfare state in Hong Kong during the transition years. It is they who most favor substantial increases in social spending. China recognizes that the expansion of social programs threatens Hong Kong's fiscal policy of low taxes and balanced budgets. Low taxes lie at the heart of Hong Kong's economic success: they are a major attraction to both foreign and domestic investors. The growth of social programs in Hong Kong might therefore jeopardize the very sources of wealth that make the colony so important to China's future plans. The Chinese, no doubt, are aware of this dilemma. It is not in their interest to inherit a debt-ridden speck of land, but they do want to gain as much popular confidence and backing as possible before 1997, subject to the economic constraint. Results from the expected utility model indicate that the policies implemented after 1997 will look significantly different from those agreed to in 1984. Once an agreement is reached, the British (and others) have diminished influence with which to prevent the Chinese from putting into practice their own policy goals. Although the Chinese are negotiating in good faith and are sincere in their intentions toward Hong Kong, the realities of internal Chinese politics will gradually force the regime to abandon the promises they set forth in the 1984 accord. Those in China most supportive of assurances for Hong Kong face stiff internal political opposition to which they will eventually yield. Here lies the resolution of China's dilemma. Internal Chinese politics, not political maneuvering in or the economic welfare of Hong Kong, dictate how the leadership in Beijing will respond to tradeoffs between economic and political goals.

IMPLEMENTATION OF THE ACCORD

The policies implemented after 1997 will not resemble the agreement signed by Britain and China. China's internal politics are so affected by decisions about Hong Kong that once the initial international settlement has been reached, ongoing reinterpretation of the accord is almost a certainty. These reinterpretations will prompt strategic responses among both Chinese and British/Hong Kong interests with substantial personal, political, or financial stakes in the future of Hong Kong. In the years up to 1997 Chinese interests will increasingly prevail because the influence of the British and local Hong Kong groups will decline steadily as a consequence of ceding sovereignty. As 1997 approaches China will be in an increasingly powerful position to implement the policies that emerge from its domestic deliberations, rather than those negotiated with Britain. The Sino—British settlement enumerates protections in the hope that it will preserve the economic and social stability of the colony. However, regardless of the explicit assurances that economic and civil freedoms will be preserved, the Chinese view of sovereignty rejects such obligations and renders them largely unenforceable. To accord such assurances as contained in the joint declaration the status of an international treaty would, in China's view, infringe on its sovereign rights.

By 1997, or soon thereafter, Hong Kong society will begin to resemble that of the People's Republic of China. It should be noted, however, that it will resemble the China of 1997, not that of today, much as today's China barely resembles the People's Republic of fourteen years ago. If, for instance, Deng's modernization program succeeds beyond current expectations, then China's policies in 1997 will be far more liberal than they are today. According to expected utility analyses of internal Chinese affairs, China's leadership will continue to come from the ranks of the modernizers. However, the commitment to modernization will not be as strong as it is today under Deng—in part because the economic sense of urgency that propels today's modernization program will likely decline as interim economic gains are achieved. Economic goals will also probably be moderated by those who will succeed Deng Xiaoping. Deng is an extremist within China on modernization questions. Consequently, it is virtually inevitable that his successors will be less willing to pursue modernization at the expense of ideological objectives. This, coupled with political infighting over modernization, is likely to make post-Deng China more conservative than it has seemed in recent years. Even if Deng succeeds in realigning forces in China so as to strengthen the hand of those who support modernization, it is unlikely that the next generation of leaders will be as strongly committed or as capable as is Deng. Thus, while we expect continued liberal reform, the pace will slow after Deng departs.

Similarly, Hong Kong in 1997 will differ from today. Economic activity will be considerably diminished from what it would have been had British rule been extended beyond 1997. Capital outflow and emigration of skilled personnel will weaken the local economy. British leverage will have diminished, and internal Chinese politics will circumscribe decisions over Hong Kong.

How do these changes affect Hong Kong's ability to remain a major manufacturing and financial center? This scenario implies a fairly straightforward rule for evaluating the prospects for foreign and locally owned businesses making long-term investment decisions. Since Hong Kong's economic system will gradually tend to resemble that of China, business firms that operate successfully on the mainland will find conditions in Hong Kong equally acceptable. Those who encounter difficulty with mainland business dealings will find Hong Kong less attractive over time. Those American firms that manufacture high-technology electronics, for instance, may not be allowed to do business in Hong Kong after 1997 because of restrictions on defense-related technology transfers to communist countries. Others will question the stability of the business environment in Chinese-ruled territory, remembering the great swings in Chinese economic policy from the Cultural Revolution to the seeming liberalization under Zhou Enlai and then Deng Xiaoping.

Hong Kong will still have important financial attractions for some time after 1997, including its extensive infrastructure and well-trained workforce. Still, the gradual transition from a free market to a more regulated economy will mean increased risks for foreign-operated business in Hong Kong. Patent and copyright laws in China are primitive and only just taking shape. Moreover, China's willingness to adhere to Western commercial law is forecast to erode as the internal political costs of accommodating such a structure increase. In time, policies in Hong Kong and in China will blend.

The evidence of a decline in Hong Kong's attractiveness to foreign investors and businesses is already emerging. At the end of February 1984, Hong Kong increased the top tax rates on personal and corporate income by two percentage points. This tax increase is the direct result of the decrease in revenues from the sale of land, whose declining value reflects fear and uncertainty about the colony's future. As a result of this tax increase, Hong Kong's attractiveness as a site for future investment must decline, leading to further shortfalls in government revenue and to potential further increases in taxes.

Still, hopeful signs appear. China is committed to economic modernization. Although they disagree on many issues, the supporters of Deng, the civil bureaucracy, and many in the military (other than the army) strongly support the preservation of Hong Kong's economic vitality to spur growth on the mainland. These prodevelopment groups are the most powerful elements in China. Though they will accommodate their opponents over the years, they are not likely to capitulate entirely. Furthermore, on some critical issues, China is not in a position to renege on the agreement. We forecast that they will accept a separate, convertible Hong Kong currency, with an independent board controlling the foreign assets that guarantee its international value. In other words, the Hong Kong dollar will be beyond China's grasp. An independent currency is a critical condition for any continuation of the Hong Kong marketplace.

Overall, the expected utility analysis shows that China will try to preserve current economic and political freedoms in Hong Kong, but that substantial pressures exist to temper those efforts. Personal freedoms will be constrained. Local citizens will control the courts, but local control means little when sovereignty resides in China. The economy will be considerably more regulated than it is now. Initially it will resemble Taiwan, but it will gradually move toward tighter regulation of commerce. Land leases will not be subject to change until their natural expiration, but at that time new leases will have to be negotiated with the Chinese. Since the model suggests they will implement a heavily regulated marketplace, it seems that considerations beyond market factors will determine rents.

In the short run, China will seek to implement the accord faithfully, retaining Hong Kong's free port and its free market economy. Investors will also take a wait-and-see attitude, tying up money only for short term projects. For the long run, investors will remain suspicious. The model suggests that the agreement has bought a short-term time horizon for stable economic conditions conducive to growth. China's good behavior each year will keep this time horizon intact; any signs of backsliding will condense it.

The maintenance of free economic institutions, a necessary condition of the territory's future prosperity, stability, and freedom, is not sufficient. If capital inflows diminish or outflows accelerate, if investment in new plant and equipment is indefinitely postponed, if entrepreneurs depart for greener pastures, and if owners of new technology are reluctant to place their processes on Chinese soil, then the rate of economic growth will slow and living standards may ultimately decline. The retention of a market economy means that Hong Kong will still make efficient use of whatever inputs it receives, but declining inputs and a lower level of entrepreneurial activity imply lower levels of output. In short, it is difficult to be optimistic that Hong Kong in the twenty-first century will repeat its economic performance of the past few decades.

In chapter 5 we displayed many of the Cartesian graphs that depict the political dynamics underlying our forecasts. While these graphs continue to be the sole source of inferences about political infighting, we dispense with their presentation here in the interest of conserving space. We continue to accompany our forecasts of policy outcomes with verbal descriptions of the political dynamics inferred from the graphs and include only especially critical graphs hereafter.

SPECIFIC ISSUE ANALYSES: 1985–1997

This section presents an issue-by-issue analysis of transition policies within Hong Kong. The next section investigates critical policy choices over Hong Kong in the domestic Chinese context. Remember, both sides will use the transition years to impose or resist efforts to establish constraints over future Chinese policies in Hong Kong. These economic, political, and social constraints can be understood in the context of detailed forecasts for the five critical issues:

> Will the free market be maintained?
> How will the tax structure change?
> How will local government evolve?
> How will wage rates and labor regulations change?
> What social welfare changes will occur?

The Free Market

Issue: What policy will be adopted toward the free market?
Forecast: The current free port and free market system with limited government intervention will be preserved through 1997.

With the exception of the government bureaucrats, all internal Hong Kong interests support the maintenance of current free

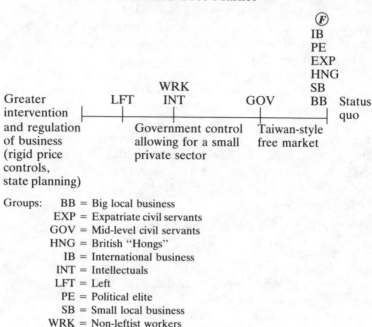

Figure 6.1
Forecast: Free Market

Groups:
- BB = Big local business
- EXP = Expatriate civil servants
- GOV = Mid-level civil servants
- HNG = British "Hongs"
- IB = International business
- INT = Intellectuals
- LFT = Left
- PE = Political elite
- SB = Small local business
- WRK = Non-leftist workers

market policies. The government bureaucrats, not surprisingly support increasing their own role by backing a small increase in government involvement in Hong Kong's business affairs. Only the workers, intellectuals, and, significantly, China's representatives in Hong Kong (hereafter called the left) call for significant increases in government direction of the economy.

The analysis shows that this is not a very contentious issue. The interests tied to Her Majesty's Government (hereafter referred to as the expatriates) are in a strong position to protect existing free market patterns in Hong Kong. The left perceives that they can challenge the expatriates: however, the expatriates will not be responsive to the leftists as they think this interest group is merely making empty demands. The evidence from the expected utility model indicates that the expatriates are correct in their view that the left cannot compel them to grant any significant concessions on this issue.

In contrast to the strong position of the expatriates, the Chinese-backed left faces serious resistance to their desire to weaken free market practices in Hong Kong. Almost all other groups expect the left to yield to pressures to continue the free market economy. The leftists are likely to harm themselves politically because of their mistaken belief that they can contest free market policies. In the end, the left must be patient. They cannot alter Hong Kong's free market direction before 1997. What China's free market practice is likely to be once they gain control is suggested by the reexamination of this issue in the next section, when internal Chinese political affairs are evaluated.

The Tax Structure

Issue: What policy will be adopted toward Hong Kong's fiscal and tax structure?
Forecast: In the transition from 1985 to 1997, the expatriate civil servants will preserve Hong Kong's low tax rates.

Apart from workers and intellectuals, all the groups favor moderate taxes for Hong Kong. The current top tax rate is 16.5 and 18.5 percent respectively for individuals and corporations. Fortunately for Hong Kong taxpayers, the workers and intel-

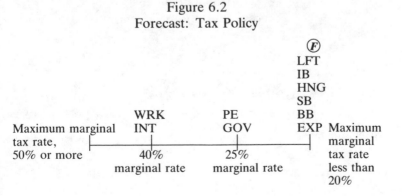

Figure 6.2
Forecast: Tax Policy

lectuals, according to the experts we consulted, have little political clout.

While the politics of taxation in Hong Kong lead, according to the expected utility model, to the maintenance of low taxes, such a forecast must be subject to the constraint of economic realities. Hong Kong has just experienced successive deficits. Funds to pay for deficits, and for deficit-inducing programs, must come from somewhere. With this caveat in mind, the forecast is for continued low taxes. The expatriates believe that their position is strong and that they need grant only small concessions to the political elite in Hong Kong and to the mid-level civil servants.

Local Government

Issue: What policy will be adopted toward local representative government?

Forecast: Hong Kong's political system will evolve into a mix of appointed and elected officials. A majority of the members of the Executive Council, Legislative Council, Urban Council and district boards will be elected. The governor will ultimately be elected by the Executive or Legislative Council. Some appointed (currently expatriate) officials, such as the highest-level civil servants, will remain, but they will be a minority.

The expatriates and left take similar positions toward the development of representative government in Hong Kong. The

Figure 6.3
Forecast: Local Representation

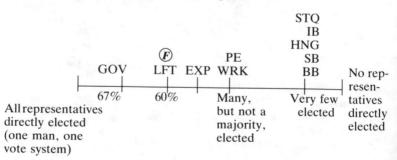

small differences they have on this issue will be resolved through the give and take of compromise politics. The real political contest is between the combined forces of the expatriates and the left on the one hand and the policy goals of business interests on the other. Hong Kong's business community will resist the development of representative government, probably because they fear the costly social welfare legislation that generally accompanies the exercise of democracy. In the end, business influence will fail to change the outcome brought about by the left and the expatriates.

Labor Regulation

Issue: What policy will be adopted toward the regulation of labor and working conditions?
Forecast: Current policies, which provide for limited government regulation of working conditions and for wage changes in response to market conditions, will begin to erode in favor of modest increases in governmental regulation.

Current policy does not regulate wages, restrict the movement of workers from one job to another, or insure job security. Only health, safety, and the number of hours women and children may work are regulated. The Hong Kong business community and the expatriate civil servants prefer the maintenance of

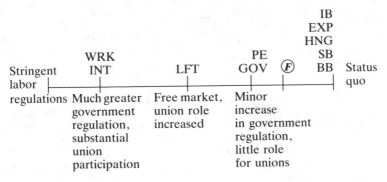

Figure 6.4[1]
Forecast: Labor Regulation

these polices, which they view as the foundation of Hong Kong's historical and future economic growth. The leftists are encouraging almost as unregulated a labor force as the political elite and mid-level civil servants for the transition years, while workers and intellectuals favor more intervention to provide greater protection and economic benefits for workers.

Those groups favoring moderate increases in regulatory policy enjoy the upper hand and they know it. The expatriates share this perspective, believing that they must yield to the wishes particularly of the leftists on this issue. However, pressure is also likely to arise from those who represent the mid-level civil servants and the political elite. These two groups, like the leftists, want to see a small increase in regulation, though they do not endorse quite as much increase as is supported by the left. The pressure for change is too great to be resisted. A compromise will be struck that gives a slight advantage to the interests of the political elite and the mid-level civil servants over the left, resulting in the small regulatory increase that we forecast.

Social Programs

Issue: What policy will be adopted toward expenditures on social programs?
Forecast: There will be a very modest increase in the size and scope of social expenditures over the twelve-year transition. These expenditures will be paid for with existing fiscal surpluses and perhaps an augmented tax structure.

Figure 6.5
Forecast: Social Welfare Expenditures

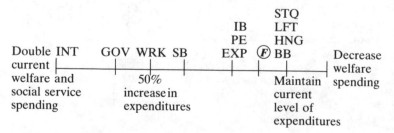

Hong Kong's policies toward social spending historically have been modest, with most expenditures limited to housing, health, and education. Although half the population lives in publicly subsidized housing, and all children are eligible for virtually free education through ninth grade, these services have been financed from a relatively small public sector that spends less than 20 percent of the gross domestic product on all public programs.

Significant differences exist on the issue of the size of social welfare programs. The Hongs, big business, and the left prefer the current arrangement. The expatriates, the political elite, and small business favor a very modest increase in social expenditures as long as the total package does not threaten the accumulated budget surplus or higher tax levels.

The expatriates believe that they will face stiff pressure from the big business interests, and less pressure from the Hongs, to retain the status quo. The expatriates believe that all other groups opposed to their policy objective either are bluffing when they state their demands or else will back off in the face of opposition. However, a wide array of concerns on both sides of the policy spectrum do not share this perception. These groups apparently believe that they can resist the demands of the expatriates and force at least some compromise with their preferred position. Thus, while they do not expect to be victorious, they are not willing to capitulate to the ambitions of the expatriates. Instead, they are prepared to hold out for a better deal which they cannot obtain. Interestingly, the only groups that actually can extract concession are those to the right of the expatriates on this issue. This will result in a very modest erosion of the status quo which moves the consequent policy between the current position and the preferred position of the expatriates.

SPECIFIC ISSUE ANALYSES: 1997 AND BEYOND

As deliberations over Hong Kong's future take place in the Crown Colony, political debate over China's post-1997 administration of Hong Kong will occur in Beijing. How will political affairs in China affect behavior toward critical issues influencing the future of Hong Kong? These are the questions that must now be resolved. The specific issues to be examined in the expected utility framework are:

> Will the free market be maintained?
> Will civil liberties be preserved?
> How independent will Hong Kong's currency be?
> Where will final judicial authority reside?
> What restrictions will be placed on foreign businesses?

The Free Market

Issue: How open a marketplace will Hong Kong be?
Forecast: As Chinese influence on this issue increases after the transfer of sovereignty in 1997, China will restrict Hong Kong's free market system. The domestic Chinese debate will result in a compromise which establishes Hong Kong as a special economic zone of China with greater economic freedom than exists in China's other special economic zones.

The Communist Party ideologues and the army in China support restricted economic incentives and limits on market forces as an appropriate foundation for socialist economic policies. Their position is consistent with contemporary Chinese practice. The bureaucrats and Guangdong faction prefer that Hong Kong be incorporated as another free-enterprise zone.

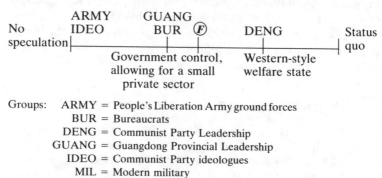

Figure 6.6
Forecast: Free Market

	ARMY IDEO	GUANG BUR ⒡	DENG	
No speculation		Government control, allowing for a small private sector	Western-style welfare state	Status quo

Groups: ARMY = People's Liberation Army ground forces
         BUR = Bureaucrats
         DENG = Communist Party Leadership
         GUANG = Guangdong Provincial Leadership
         IDEO = Communist Party ideologues
         MIL = Modern military

Throughout the analysis it appears that the Guangdong leadership takes self-interested positions intended to restrict the competitive advantage of Hong Kong over Guangdong Province. Deng wants to establish a special status for Hong Kong, an extremist position within China. This policy involves controls on vice and some limits on "excessive" speculation, but preserves significant market forces.

The analysis shows that the modernizers have seriously misperceived their ability to implement either Deng's policies or the international agreement to which China will be a party. As is evident from figure 6.7, the modernizers believe they can resist

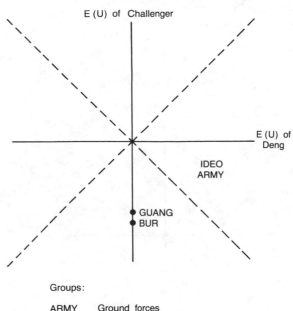

Figure 6.7

Free Market: Perspective of Deng's Successors

Groups:

ARMY	Ground forces
BUR	Bureaucrats
DENG	Communist Party leadership (Deng's successors)
GUANG	Guangdong Provincial leadership
IDEO	Communist Party ideologues
MIL	Modern military (air / navy / missile)

the demands of the ideologues and army and that the bureaucrats and the Guangdong Provincial leadership will yield to their demands. However, these groups, as seen in figure 6.8, believe they can successfully counter the modernizers' attempts to establish a "regulated free market." Such perceptions will produce costly mistakes for Deng's successors among the modernizers. The opponents of Deng's rapid modernization program can force an outcome which begins the process of transforming Hong Kong's economy to look like a Chinese special economic zone. Deng's successors simply are not prepared to pay as high a price to preserve the free market as the Party ideologues, the bureaucracy, and the GPL are to modify the policy away from the spirit of the agreement. Thus, domestic pressures will ultimately force Deng's successors to compromise with those seeking a more regulated economic system than anticipated by the international accords.

Figure 6.8

Free Market: Challenger's Perspective

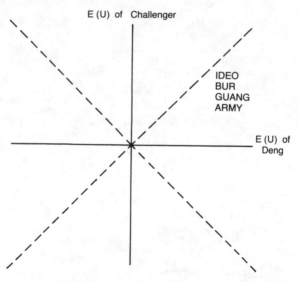

Figure 6.9
Forecast: Civil Liberties

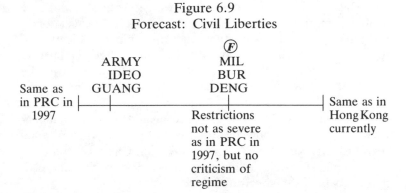

Civil Liberties

Issue: What policy will be adopted toward civil liberties in Hong Kong?
Forecast: The domestic Chinese resolution of this issue produces the most liberal Chinese alternative. Even this position, however, retreats from the Western-style individual rights policy set out in the international accords.

Deng's supporters take the most liberal position on civil liberties of any group in China. They would prohibit criticism of the government, but they are willing to permit greater freedom for Hong Kong residents than for their mainland counterparts. Deng and the modernizers are opposed by the ideologues, the army, and Guangdong faction, groups which prefer merging Hong Kong into China. The model reveals that Deng's successors will face only mild opposition from these three groups (in fact, the GPL is likely to capitulate on this issue in the face of any pressure from Deng), and they will, therefore, be able to impose their will.

The Judicial System

Issue: What policy will be adopted toward the court system?
Forecast: With the transfer of sovereignty in 1997 and the ultimate resolution of this issue within the Chinese political system, the courts will remain under local control.

This is one of the few issues on which Deng does not face serious domestic political challenges to his goals. Localization of the judiciary can be consistent with the Chinese objective of unfettered sovereignty. Consequently, this policy can survive both international and domestic challenges. Although the model does not address desires within China for consistent judicial practices, we speculate that, with time, political pressures for judicial consistency between Hong Kong and conventional Chinese practice may erode the autonomy of purely Western practices in Hong Kong's courts, assuming that China continues to use its judicial system to advance the political, social, and economic goals of the government.

Figure 6.10
Forecast: Courts

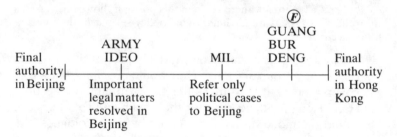

The Hong Kong Dollar

Issue: What policy will be adopted toward the Hong Kong currency and convertibility?
Forecast: While credible internal domestic pressure exists for the Bank of China to control Hong Kong's currency reserves, the existence of an independent currency board will prevent this from occurring. If the board were not isolated from internal political dynamics, China would use the reserves in pursuit of its own internal goals.

Figure 6.11
Forecast: Currency

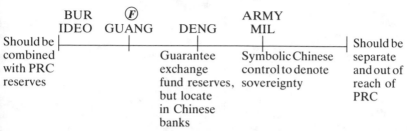

Within China, the ideologues and bureaucracy want to use the Hong Kong reserves for such domestic purposes as economic development and modernization. They view this as a very important issue on their Hong Kong agenda. Deng's domestic position is for the Bank of China to manage the reserves to support a Hong Kong currency. This reflects his willingness to limit China's role in Hong Kong. If the international agreement did not assure the existence of an independent currency board, the Chinese would adopt the policy supported by the Guangdong Provincial leadership. They call for partial absorption of Hong Kong's assets into China's reserves. The bureaucrats, assisted by the ideologues and the GPL, can (as seen in figures 6.12 and 6.13) force Deng's successors to accept greater Chinese control and use of the Hong Kong reserves than they view as desirable or prudent.

In the absence of an independent currency board, Chinese control of Hong Kong's reserves would damage international confidence. Domestic political pressures would force China to use the reserves for purposes other than backing the Hong Kong currency. The forecast implies that opponents of Deng's modernization program will seize any opportunity to gain greater control over Hong Kong's currency after 1997. One can only speculate on their likelihood of success. The forecast calls our attention to the importance of watching how the currency board's relationship with the Chinese government evolves.

Figure 6.12

Currency: Perspective of Deng's Successors

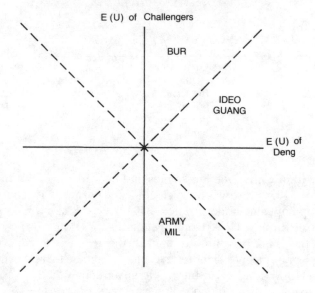

Figure 6.13

Currency: Challenger's Perspective

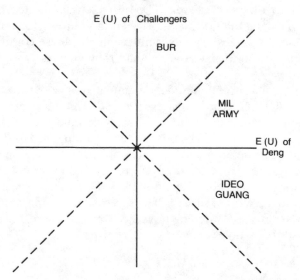

Regulation of Foreign Business

Issue: What operating restrictions on foreign businesses in Hong Kong will be adopted?

Forecast: Deng has declared that no operating restrictions will be imposed on foreign businesses located in Hong Kong. His coalition will be able to defend this policy within the domestic environment.

Deng and the bureaucracy want to use Hong Kong as a vehicle for modernizing and promoting further development of the mainland. Conversely, the ideologues and army object to the notion of according special treatment to Hong Kong. Finally, the Guangdong leadership prefers restrictions on foreign business that limit Hong Kong's competition with Guangdong Province as a site for investment.

The analysis indicates that the modernizing coalition, which includes Deng's successors and the bureaucracy, will endure the pressure from the ideologues and successfully resist attempts to impose restrictions on the operation of foreign businesses.

Figure 6.14
Forecast: Foreign Business Restrictions

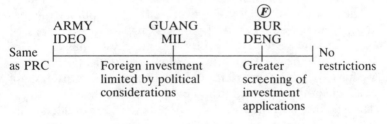

7
Expected Utility Forecasting: A Better Mousetrap?

How are we to know a better mousetrap when we see one? The answer is simple! The better mousetrap catches more mice. How are we to know a better way of analyzing politics? The answer again is simple! The better theory explains and predicts more facts. Is the expected utility theory a better way of analyzing politics? Although each reader must make his or her own judgment, two qualities make the expected utility approach an extremely attractive method of political analysis.

Mathematicized political models are mysterious creatures that often appear intimidating. To overcome this impediment, we have tried in chapter 2 to set forth in straightforward fashion the logic in the expected utility model and the data it requires. Thus neither the theory's logic nor its data are hidden from view. Assumptions are explicit and their purpose and meaning are explained. The data used are equally explicit and the future orientation of its predictions precludes rationalizations that make the facts appear to fit the theory. After all, many of the predictions concern events that will not transpire until the end of this century. Earlier, we said we hope to persuade by example. Now our example can be reviewed and evaluated.

Chapter 5 investigated the Sino−British negotiations over the future of Hong Kong. All of that analysis was completed and

disseminated by Data Resources Incorporated/Policon Corporation for commercial clients in March 1984, months before the
relevant events took place. The analysis relies solely on the logic
of the expected utility model and appropriate data based on the
knowledge of leading experts. Inferences about the negotiations
follow directly from the characterization of politics as a rational,
issue-oriented competition among interest groups who seek to
maximize expected utility. Although experts provided the data
on group preferences, resources, and salience, they did not
supply forecasts or interpret the model's results. The forecasts in
chapter 5 accurately reflect the terms of the agreement (reprinted
in the appendix to this volume).

Social scientists are, by nature, skeptics. And this is as it
should be. Consequently, some will say that success in predicting
the results of the Sino – British negotiations was luck or was easy.
Others will say the results are precisely what any good expert
would have forecast, inferring that a model was not necessary,
just expertise and common sense. For those skeptics there is
chapter 6. There, events that have yet to happen are forecast
with the same precision and detail as are the terms of the
agreement. Already tidbits about relevant political competition
within China have begun to leak out. The newspapers speculate
that Deng faces unanticipated, stiff opposition from China's
conservatives, and that this opposition is making him take a hard
line. Deng's announcement in early summer, 1984, that China
will billet troops in Hong Kong was taken by journalists as a sign
that the struggle between the modernizers and the ideologues is
less onesided than had been thought. That struggle is clearly
anticipated in the expected utility results. Indeed, it is described
in much greater detail than is yet possible from journalistic
accounts of events in China. Likewise, some of the maneuvering
in Hong Kong anticipated by the analysis is becoming visible.
But the forecasts extend well beyond these smatterings of evidence from the real world. Students of politics can take a long,
slow look at the forecasts, which may be compared with reality
for years to come.

Good theory does not guarantee correct forecasts. The further into the future one forecasts, the more likely that data

assumptions will go astray. Deng, over eighty, will not be a factor in 1997. Whether his followers and supporters will have the political savvy or personal charisma to retain his influence can only be guessed. The expected utility theory does not illuminate such changes in political influence as are brought about by events outside the scope of the model, for example, the untimely death of a leader. A new key actor may bring different preferences, resources, and salience to bear on an issue, thus generating new outcomes. Similarly, the theory does not inquire into the origins of preferences; it only depends on knowing issue preferences to make predictions. As economists are fond of saying, "there is no accounting for taste." But experience shows that preferences on significant matters do not rapidly change.

The expected utility model is robust. Changes in one or another group's preferences often do not significantly alter either the predicted policy choice or the degree of contentiousness surrounding it. One of the model's great strengths is its ability to simulate the effects of real or hypothetical changes in preferences, power, or salience. The ability to simulate alternative circumstances provides an opportunity to assess and reassess forecasts. We have made educated guesses about future states of the world in constructing the data assumptions for chapter 6. As better information becomes available, new analyses can and should be done.

Similarly, simulations of alternative group strategies can be done. What, if anything, can Deng, the expatriates, or the Hong Kong business community do to improve policy choices from their standpoint? Would shifting their apparent stance on an issue or committing more resources help or hinder their prospects for success? Would moderation or greater extremism be more likely to foster political compromises favorable to their objectives? These are not questions with obvious or universal answers. Sometimes seemingly extremist behavior weakens one's position, alienating important centrist groups, but at other times it draws together fractionalized elements on the right or the left. There is not always a better strategy for a group, but when there is, the expected utility approach shows what it is, what can be gained, and at what cost.

The theory set forth here is in the spirit of a truly predictive science of politics. It is powerful, parsimonious, and flexible, with an ostensibly successful track record. But the model is amenable to further refinement and work is underway to amplify its capabilities. First, for the model presented in this book, current forecasts are about individual issues. The many facets of important political questions are collapsed onto a one-dimensional continuum. The opportunities for logrolling are ignored; there is no discussion of possible trades and compromises across issues. Some questions, of course, are not one-dimensional. Ultimately, a better view of politics will take into account how issues are connected to one another.

Second, the model does not yet identify a way to approximate the implications of spending resources on one issue for the availability of resources on other issues. Can success on one issue lead to an increase in resources available for achieving goals on other issues, or are sunk costs sunk in politics as in economics? Resources are not unlimited. Does a concerted effort on one question enhance or harm one's prospects on future or concurrent questions? Can the theoretical problem of tradeoffs between issues be solved? The answer as of now is unclear. This is akin to the microeconomist's problem of measuring marginal rates of substitution in a world of unknown, but real, budget constraints. The solution will reveal whether sincere or sophisticated expressions of salience are the norm in politics. For now, we must assume sincere behavior with regard to salience (though not with regard to preferences).

Third, the model presented here does not include estimates of future policy decisions when the target group makes no attempt to impose its goals. More recent elaborations of the model have solved this problem. One can calculate, in part by using Black's median voter theorem, the expected utility of inaction even when the status quo is not expected to continue. Fourth, the current model provides an explanation of each of the octants of the Cartesian graphs defined by the expected utility values. However, no differentiation between separate points in the same octant is possible. This problem too has been addressed in more recent elaborations of the theory. Notwithstanding these four theoretical limitations of the model developed here, it has proven remarkably successful as a tool for explaining and forecasting political decisions.

The problems of data reliability in a theory that depends on measuring individual utilities are great indeed. Standardized sources of information simply do not exist. The predictive power of any approach whether grounded in a formal model, statistical curve fitting, or expert judgment, is only as good as the information that goes into it. Fortunately, superb expertise on individual countries, regions, and issue-areas is readily available within the academic, government, and business communities. While lapses in the quality of data will, from time to time, produce wrong forecasts, at least one can be confident that the best available information is used. Consequently, with the advantages of a systematic, powerful expected utility model for forecasting, we should expect future political analyses to be superior to those done in the past. The flaws in the data may persist, but the procedure for evaluating the data has been improved.

We have put our attempt to develop a predictive science of politics and policy formation in clear view. Can it stand the test of time?

Appendix: Sino-British Joint Declaration on the Question of Hong Kong

JOINT DECLARATION OF THE GOVERNMENT OF THE UNITED KINGDOM OF GREAT BRITAIN AND NORTHERN IRELAND AND THE GOVERNMENT OF THE PEOPLE'S REPUBLIC OF CHINA ON THE QUESTION OF HONG KONG

The Government of the United Kingdom of Great Britain and Northern Ireland and the Government of the People's Republic of China have reviewed with satisfaction the friendly relations existing between the two Governments and peoples in recent years and agreed that a proper negotiated settlement of the question of Hong Kong, which is left over from the past, is conducive to the maintenance of the prosperity and stability of Hong Kong and to the further strengthening and development of the relations between the two countries on a new basis. To this end, they have, after talks between the delegations of the two Governments, agreed to declare as follows:

1. The Government of the People's Republic of China declares that to recover the Hong Kong area (including Hong Kong Island, Kowloon and the New Territories, hereinafter referred to as Hong Kong) is the common aspiration of the entire Chinese people, and that it has decided to resume the exercise of sovereignty over Hong Kong with effect from 1 July 1997.

2. The Government of the United Kingdom declares that it will restore Hong Kong to the People's Republic of China with effect from 1 July 1997.

3. The Government of the People's Republic of China de-

clares that the basic policies of the People's Republic of China regarding Hong Kong are as follows:

(1) Upholding national unity and territorial integrity and taking account of the history of Hong Kong and its realities, the People's Republic of China has decided to establish, in accordance with the provisions of Article 31 of the Constitution of the People's Republic of China, a Hong Kong Special Administrative Region upon resuming the exercise of sovereignty over Hong Kong.

(2) The Hong Kong Special Administrative Region will be directly under the authority of the Central People's Government of the People's Republic of China. The Hong Kong Special Administrative Region will enjoy a high degree of autonomy, except in foreign and defence affairs which are the responsibilities of the Central People's Government.

(3) The Hong Kong Special Administrative Region will be vested with executive, legislative and independent judicial power, including that of final adjudication. The laws currently in force in Hong Kong will remain basically unchanged.

(4) The Government of the Hong Kong Special Administrative Region will be composed of local inhabitants. The chief executive will be appointed by the Central People's Government on the basis of the results of elections or consultations to be held locally. Principal officials will be nominated by the chief executive of the Hong Kong Special Administrative Region for appointment by the Central People's Government. Chinese and foreign nationals previously working in the public and police services in the government departments of Hong Kong may remain in employment. British and other foreign nationals may also be employed to serve as advisers or hold certain public posts in government departments of the Hong Kong Special Administrative Region.

(5) The current social and economic systems in Hong Kong will remain unchanged, and so will the life-style. Rights and freedoms, including those of the person, of speech, of the press, of assembly, of association, of travel, of movement, of correspondence, of strike, of choice of occupation, of academic research and of religious belief will be ensured by law in the Hong Kong Special Administrative Region. Private property, ownership of enterprises, legitimate right of inheritance and foreign investment will be protected by law.

(6) The Hong Kong Special Administrative Region will retain the status of a free port and a separate customs territory.

(7) The Hong Kong Special Administrative Region will retain the

status of an international financial centre, and its markets for foreign exchange, gold, securities and futures will continue. There will be free flow of capital. The Hong Kong dollar will continue to circulate and remain freely convertible.

(8) The Hong Kong Special Administrative Region will have independent finances. The Central People's Government will not levy taxes on the Hong Kong Special Administrative Region.

(9) The Hong Kong Special Administrative Region may establish mutually beneficial economic relations with the United Kingdom and other countries, whose economic interests in Hong Kong will be given due regard.

(10) Using the name of "Hong Kong, China", the Hong Kong Special Administrative Region may on its own maintain and develop economic and cultural relations and conclude relevant agreements with states, regions and relevant international organisations. The Government of the Hong Kong Special Administrative Region may on its own issue travel documents for entry into and exit from Hong Kong.

(11) The maintenance of public order in the Hong Kong Special Administrative Region will be the responsibility of the Government of the Hong Kong Special Administrative Region.

(12) The above-stated basic policies of the People's Republic of China regarding Hong Kong and the elaboration of them in Annex I to this Joint Declaration will be stipulated, in a Basic Law of the Hong Kong Special Administrative Region of the People's Republic of China, by the National People's Congress of the People's Republic of China, and they will remain unchanged for 50 years.

4. The Government of the United Kingdom and the Government of the People's Republic of China declare that, during the transitional period between the date of the entry into force of this Joint Declaration and 30 June 1997, the Government of the United Kingdom will be responsible for the administration of Hong Kong with the object of preserving its economic prosperity and social stability; and that the Government of the People's Republic of China will give its cooperation in this connection.

5. The Government of the United Kingdom and the Government of the People's Republic of China declare that, in order to ensure a smooth transfer of government in 1997, and with a view to the effective implementation of this Joint Declaration, a

Sino-British Joint Liaison Group will be set up when this Joint Declaration enters into force; and that it will be established and will function in accordance with the provisions of Annex II to this Joint Declaration.

6. The Government of the United Kingdom and the Government of the People's Republic of China declare that land leases in Hong Kong and other related matters will be dealt with in accordance with the provisions of Annex III to this Joint Declaration.

7. The Government of the United Kingdom and the Government of the People's Republic of China agree to implement the preceding declaration and the Annexes to this Joint Declaration.

8. This Joint Declaration is subject to ratification and shall enter into force on the date of the exchange of instruments of ratification, which shall take place in Beijing before 30 June 1985. This Joint Declaration and its Annexes shall be equally binding.

Done in duplicate at Beijing on   1984 in the English and Chinese languages, both texts being equally authentic.

(Signed)
For the Government of
the United Kingdom of
Great Britain and
Northern Ireland

(Signed)
For the Government of
the People's Republic
of China

ANNEX I
ELABORATION BY THE GOVERNMENT OF THE PEOPLE'S REPUBLIC OF CHINA OF ITS BASIC POLICIES REGARDING HONG KONG

The Government of the People's Republic of China elaborates the basic policies of the People's Republic of China regarding Hong Kong as set out in paragraph 3 of the Joint Declaration of the Government of the United Kingdom of Great Britain and Northern Ireland and the Government of the People's Republic of China on the Question of Hong Kong as follows:

I

The Constitution of the People's Republic of China stipulates in Article 31 that "the state may establish special administrative regions when necessary. The systems to be instituted in special administrative regions shall be prescribed by laws enacted by the National People's Congress in the light of specific conditions." In accordance with this Article, the People's Republic of China shall, upon the resumption of the exercise of sovereignty over Hong Kong on 1 July 1997, establish the Hong Kong Special Administrative Region of the People's Republic of China. The National People's Congress of the People's Republic of China shall enact and promulgate a Basic Law of the Hong Kong Special Administrative Region of the People's Republic of China (hereinafter referred to as the Basic Law) in accordance with the

Constitution of the People's Republic of China, stipulating that after the establishment of the Hong Kong Special Administrative Region the socialist system and socialist policies shall not be practiced in the Hong Kong Special Administrative Region and that Hong Kong's previous capitalist system and life-style shall remain unchanged for 50 years.

The Hong Kong Special Administrative Region shall be directly under the authority of the Central People's Government of the People's Republic of China and shall enjoy a high degree of autonomy. Except for foreign and defence affairs which are the responsibilities of the Central People's Government, the Hong Kong Special Administrative Region shall be vested with executive, legislative and independent judicial power, including that of final adjudication. The Central People's Government shall authorise the Hong Kong Special Administrative Region to conduct on its own those external affairs specified in Section XI of this Annex.

The government and legislature of the Hong Kong Special Administrative Region shall be selected by election or through consultations held locally and be appointed by the Central People's Government. Principal officials (equivalent to Secretaries) shall be nominated by the chief executive of the Hong Kong Special Administrative Region and appointed by the Central People's Government. The legislature of the Hong Kong Special Administrative Region shall be constituted by elections. The executive authorities shall abide by the law and shall be accountable to the legislature.

In addition to Chinese, English may also be used in organs of government and in the courts in the Hong Kong Special Administrative Region.

Apart from displaying the national flag and national emblem of the People's Republic of China, the Hong Kong Special Administrative Region may use a regional flag and emblem of its own.

II

After the establishment of the Hong Kong Special Administrative Region, the laws previously in force in Hong Kong (i.e.

the common law, rules of equity, ordinances, subordinate legislation and customary law) shall be maintained, save for any that contravene the Basic Law and subject to any amendment by the Hong Kong Special Administrative Region legislature.

The legislative power of the Hong Kong Special Administrative Region shall be vested in the legislature of the Hong Kong Special Administrative Region. The legislature may on its own authority enact laws in accordance with the provisions of the Basic Law and legal procedures, and report them to the Standing Committee of the National People's Congress for the record. Laws enacted by the legislature which are in accordance with the Basic Law and legal procedures shall be regarded as valid.

The laws of the Hong Kong Special Administrative Region shall be the Basic Law, and the laws previously in force in Hong Kong and laws enacted by the Hong Kong Special Administrative Region legislature as above.

III

After the establishment of the Hong Kong Special Administrative Region, the judicial system previously practised in Hong Kong shall be maintained except for those changes consequent upon the vesting in the courts of the Hong Kong Special Administrative Region of the power of final adjudication.

Judicial power in the Hong Kong Special Administrative Region shall be vested in the courts of the Hong Kong Special Administrative Region. The courts shall exercise judicial power independently and free from any interference. Members of the judiciary shall be immune from legal action in respect of their judicial functions. The courts shall decide cases in accordance with the laws of the Hong Kong Special Administrative Region and may refer to precedents in other common law jurisdictions.

Judges of the Hong Kong Special Administrative Region courts shall be appointed by the chief executive of the Hong Kong Special Administrative Region acting in accordance with the recommendation of an independent commission composed of local judges, persons from the legal profession and other eminent persons. Judges shall be chosen by reference to their judicial qualities and may be recruited from other common law jurisdictions. A judge may only be removed for inability to discharge the functions of office, or for misbehaviour, by the chief executive of the Hong Kong Special Administrative Region acting in accordance with the recommendation of a tribunal appointed by the chief judge of the court of final appeal, consisting of not fewer than three local judges. Additionally, the appointment or removal of principal judges (i.e. those of the highest rank) shall be made by the chief executive with the endorsement of the Hong Kong Special Administrative Region legislature and reported to the Standing Committee of the National People's Congress for the record. The system of appointment and removal of judicial officers other than judges shall be maintained.

The power of final judgment of the Hong Kong Special Administrative Region shall be vested in the court of final appeal in the Hong Kong Special Administrative Region, which may as required invite judges from other common law jurisdictions to sit on the court of final appeal.

A prosecuting authority of the Hong Kong Special Administrative Region shall control criminal prosecutions free from any interference.

On the basis of the system previously operating in Hong Kong, the Hong Kong Special Administrative Region Government shall on its own make provision for local lawyers and lawyers from outside the Hong Kong Special Administrative Region to work and practise in the Hong Kong Special Administrative Region.

The Central People's Government shall assist or authorise the Hong Kong Special Administrative Region Government to make appropriate arrangements for reciprocal juridical assistance with foreign states.

IV

After the establishment of the Hong Kong Special Administrative Region, public servants previously serving in Hong Kong in all government departments, including the police department, and members of the judiciary may all remain in employment and continue their service with pay, allowances, benefits and conditions of service no less favourable than before. The Hong Kong Special Administrative Region Government shall pay to such persons who retire or complete their contracts, as well as to those who have retired before 1 July 1997, or to their dependents, all pensions, gratuities, allowances and benefits due to them on terms no less favourable than before, and irrespective of their nationality or place of residence.

The Hong Kong Special Administrative Region Government may employ British and other foreign nationals previously serving in the public service in Hong Kong, and may recruit British and other foreign nationals holding permanent identity cards of the Hong Kong Special Administrative Region to serve as public servants at all levels, except as heads of major government departments (corresponding to branches or departments at Secretary level) including the police department, and as deputy heads of some of those departments. The Hong Kong Special Administrative Region Government may also employ British and other foreign nationals as advisers to government departments and, when there is a need, may recruit qualified candidates from outside the Hong Kong Special Administrative Region to professional and technical posts in government departments. The above shall be employed only in their individual capacities and, like other public servants, shall be responsible to the Hong Kong Special Administrative Region Government.

The appointment and promotion of public servants shall be on the basis of qualifications, experience and ability. Hong Kong's previous system of recruitment, employment, assessment, discipline, training and management for the public service (including special bodies for appointment, pay and conditions of service) shall, save for any provisions providing privileged treatment for foreign nationals, be maintained.

V

The Hong Kong Special Administrative Region shall deal on its own with financial matters, including disposing of its financial resources and drawing up its budgets and its final accounts. The Hong Kong Special Administrative Region shall report its budgets and final accounts to the Central People's Government for the record.

The Central People's Government shall not levy taxes on the Hong Kong Special Administrative Region. The Hong Kong Special Administrative Region shall use its financial revenues exclusively for its own purposes and they shall not be handed over to the Central People's Government. The systems by which taxation and by which there is accountability to the legislature for all public expenditure, and the system for auditing public accounts shall be maintained.

VI

The Hong Kong Special Administrative Region shall maintain the capitalist economic and trade systems previously practised in Hong Kong. The Hong Kong Special Administrative Region Government shall decide its economic and trade policies on its own. Rights concerning the ownership of property, including those relating to acquisition, use, disposal, inheritance and compensation for lawful deprivation (corresponding to the real value of the property concerned, freely convertible and paid without undue delay) shall continue to be protected by law.

The Hong Kong Special Administrative Region shall retain the status of a free port and continue a free trade policy, including the free movement of goods and capital. The Hong Kong Special Administrative Region may on its own maintain and develop economic and trade relations with all states and regions.

The Hong Kong Special Administrative Region shall be a separate customs territory. It may participate in relevant international organisations and international trade agreements (including preferential trade arrangements), such as the General Agreement on Tariffs and Trade and arrangements regarding international trade in textiles. Export quotas, tariff preferences and other similar arrangements obtained by the Hong Kong Special Administrative Region shall be enjoyed exclusively by the Hong Kong Special Administrative Region. The Hong Kong Special

Administrative Region shall have authority to issue its own certificates of origin for products manufactured locally, in accordance with prevailing rules of origin.

The Hong Kong Special Administrative Region may, as necessary, establish official and semi-official economic and trade missions in foreign countries, reporting the establishment of such missions to the Central People's Government for the record.

VII

The Hong Kong Special Administrative Region shall retain the status of an international financial centre. The monetary and financial systems previously practised in Hong Kong, including the systems of regulation and supervision of deposit taking institutions and financial markets, shall be maintained.

The Hong Kong Special Administrative Region Government may decide its monetary and financial policies on its own. It shall safeguard the free operation of financial business and the free flow of capital within, into and out of the Hong Kong Special Administrative Region. No exchange control policy shall be applied in the Hong Kong Special Administrative Region. Markets for foreign exchange, gold, securities and futures shall continue.

The Hong Kong dollar, as the local legal tender, shall continue to circulate and remain freely convertible. The authority to issue Hong Kong currency shall be vested in the Hong Kong Special Administrative Region Government. The Hong Kong Special Administrative Region Government may authorise designated banks to issue or continue to issue Hong Kong currency under statutory authority, after satisfying itself that any issue of currency will be soundly based and that the arrangements for such issue are consistent with the object of maintaining the stability of the currency. Hong Kong currency bearing references inappropriate to the status of Hong Kong as a Special Administrative Region of the People's Republic of China shall be progressively replaced and withdrawn from circulation.

The Exchange Fund shall be managed and controlled by the Hong Kong Special Administrative Region Government, primarily for regulating the exchange value of the Hong Kong dollar.

VIII

The Hong Kong Special Administrative Region shall maintain Hong Kong's previous systems of shipping management and shipping regulation, including the system for regulating conditions of seamen. The specific functions and responsibilities of the Hong Kong Special Administrative Region Government in the field of shipping shall be defined by the Hong Kong Special Administrative Region Government on its own. Private shipping businesses and shipping-related businesses and private container terminals in Hong Kong may continue to operate freely.

The Hong Kong Special Administrative Region shall be authorised by the Central People's Government to continue to maintain a shipping register and issue related certificates under its own legislation in the name of "Hong Kong, China".

With the exception of foreign warships, access for which requires the permission of the Central People's Government, ships shall enjoy access to the ports of the Hong Kong Special Administrative Region in accordance with the laws of the Hong Kong Special Administrative Region.

IX

The Hong Kong Special Administrative Region shall maintain the status of Hong Kong as a centre of international and regional aviation. Airlines incorporated and having their principal place of business in Hong Kong and civil aviation related businesses may continue to operate. The Hong Kong Special Administrative Region shall continue the previous system of civil aviation management in Hong Kong, and keep its own aircraft register in accordance with provisions laid down by the Central People's Government concerning nationality marks of aircraft. The Hong Kong Special Administrative Region shall be responsible on its own for matters of routine business and technical management of civil aviation, including the management of airports, the provision of air traffic services within the flight information region of the Hong Kong Special Administrative Region, and the discharge of other responsibilities allocated under the regional air navigation procedures of the International Civil Aviation Organisation.

The Central People's Government shall, in consultation with the Hong Kong Special Administrative Region Government, make arrangements providing for air services between the Hong Kong Special Administrative Region and other parts of the People's Republic of China for airlines incorporated and having their principal place of business in the Hong Kong Special Administrative Region and other airlines of the People's Republic of China. All Air Service Agreements providing for air services between other parts of the People's Republic of China and other states and regions with stops at the Hong Kong Special Administrative Region and air services between the Hong Kong Special Administrative Region and other states and regions with stops at other parts of the People's Republic of China shall be concluded by the Central People's Government. For this purpose, the Central People's Government shall take account of the special conditions and economic interests of the Hong Kong Special Administrative Region Government. Representatives of the Hong Kong Special Administrative Region Government may participate as members of delegations of the Government of the People's Republic of China in air service consultations with foreign governments concerning arrangements for such services.

Acting under specific authorisations from the Central People's Government, the Hong Kong Special Administrative Region Government may:

—renew or amend Air Service Agreements and arrangements previously in force; in principle, all such Agreements and arrangements may be renewed or amended with the rights contained in such previous Agreements and arrangements being as far as possible maintained;
—negotiate and conclude new Air Service Agreements providing routes for airlines incorporated and having their principal place of business in the Hong Kong Special Administrative Region and rights for overflights and technical stops; and
—negotiate and conclude provisional arrangements where no Air Service Agreement with a foreign state or other region is in force.

All scheduled air services to, from or through the Hong Kong Special Administrative Region which do not operate to, from or through the mainland of China shall be regulated by Air

Service Agreements or provisional arrangements referred to in the paragraph.

The Central People's Government shall give the Hong Kong Special Administrative Region Government the authority to:

—negotiate and conclude with other authorities all arrangements concerning the implementation of the above Air Service Agreements and provisional arrangements;
—issue licences to airlines incorporated and having their principal place of business in the Hong Kong Special Administrative Region;
—designate such airlines under the above Air Service Agreements and provisional arrangements; and
—issue permits to foreign airlines for services other than those to, from or through the mainland of China.

X

The Hong Kong Special Administrative Region shall maintain the educational system previously practised in Hong Kong. The Hong Kong Special Administrative Region Government shall on its own decide policies in the fields of culture, education, science and technology, including policies regarding the educational system and its administration, the language of instruction, the allocation of funds, the examination system, the system of academic awards and the recognition of educational and technological qualifications. Institutions of all kinds, including those run by religious and community organisations, may retain their autonomy. They may continue to recruit staff and use teaching materials from outside the Hong Kong Special Administrative Region. Students shall enjoy freedom of choice of education and freedom to pursue their education outside the Hong Kong Special Administrative Region.

XI

Subject to the principle that foreign affairs are the responsibility of the Central People's Government, representatives of the Hong Kong Special Administrative Region Government may participate, as members of delegations of the Government of the People's Republic of China, in negotiations at the diplomatic level directly affecting the Hong Kong Special Administrative Region conducted by the Central People's Government. The Hong Kong Special Administrative Region may on its own, using the name "Hong Kong, China", maintain and develop relations and conclude and implement agreements with states, regions and relevant international organisations in the appropriate fields, including the economic, trade, financial and monetary, shipping, communications, touristic, cultural and sporting fields. Representatives of the Hong Kong Special Administrative Region Government may participate, as members of delegations of the Government of the People's Republic of China, in international organisations or conferences in appropriate fields limited to states and affecting the Hong Kong Special Administrative Region, or may attend in such other capacity as may be permitted by the Central People's Government and the organisation or conference concerned, and may express their views in the name of "Hong Kong, China". The Hong Kong Special Administrative Region may, using the name "Hong Kong, China", participate in international organisations and conferences not limited to states.

The application to the Hong Kong Special Administrative Region of international agreements to which the People's Republic of China is or becomes a party shall be decided by the Central People's Government, in accordance with the circumstances and needs of the Hong Kong Special Administrative Region, and after seeking the views of the Hong Kong Special Administrative Region Government. International agreements to which the People's Republic of China is not a party but which are implemented in Hong Kong may remain implemented in the Hong Kong Special Administrative Region. The Central People's Government shall, as necessary, authorise or assist the Hong Kong Special Administrative Region Government to make appropriate arrangements for the application to the Hong Kong Special Administrative Region of other relevant international agreements. The Central People's Government shall take the necessary steps to ensure that the Hong Kong Special Administrative Region shall continue to retain its status in an appropriate capacity in those international organisations of which Hong Kong participates in one capacity or another. The Central People's ment shall, where necessary, facilitate the continued participation of the Hong Kong Special Administrative Region in an appropriate capacity in those international organisations in which Hong Kong is a participant in one capacity or another, but of which the People's Republic of China is not a member.

Foreign consular and other official or semi-official missions may be established in the Hong Kong Special Administrative Region with the approval of the Central People's Government. Consular and other official missions established in Hong Kong by states which have established formal diplomatic relations with the People's Republic of China may be maintained. According to the circumstances of each case, consular and other official missions of states having no formal diplomatic relations with the People's Republic of China may either be maintained or changed to semi-official missions. States not recognised by the People's Republic of China can only establish non-governmental institutions.

The United Kingdom may establish a Consulate-General in the Hong Kong Special Administrative Region.

XII

The maintenance of public order in the Hong Kong Special Administrative Region shall be the responsibility of the Hong Kong Special Administrative Region Government. Military forces sent by the Central People's Government to be stationed in the Hong Kong Special Administrative Region for the purpose of defence shall not interfere in the internal affairs of the Hong Kong Special Administrative Region. Expenditure for these military forces shall be borne by the Central People's Government.

XIII

The Hong Kong Special Administrative Region Government shall protect the rights and freedoms of inhabitants and other persons in the Hong Kong Special Administrative Region according to law. The Hong Kong Special Administrative Region Government shall maintain the rights and freedoms as provided for the laws previously in force in Hong Kong, including freedom of the person, of speech, of the press, of assembly, of association, to form and join trade unions, of correspondence, of travel, of movement, of strike, of demonstration, of choice of occupation, of academic research, of belief, inviolability of the home, the freedom to marry and the right to raise a family freely.

Every person shall have the right to confidential legal advice, access to the courts, representation in the courts by lawyers of his choice, and to obtain judicial remedies. Every person shall have the right to challenge the actions of the executive in the courts.

Religious organisations and believers may maintain their relations with religious organisations and believers elsewhere, and schools, hospitals and welfare institutions run by religious organisations in the Hong Kong Special Administrative Region and those in other parts of the People's Republic of China shall be based on the principles of non-subordination, non-interference and mutual respect.

The provisions of the International Covenant on Civil and Political Rights and the International Covenant on Economic, Social and Cultural Rights as applied to Hong Kong shall remain in force.

XIV

The following categories of persons shall have the right of abode in the Hong Kong Special Administrative Region, and, in accordance with the law of the Hong Kong Special Administrative Region, be qualified to obtain permanent identity cards issued by the Hong Kong Special Administrative Region Government, which state their right of abode:

—all Chinese nationals who were born or who have ordinarily resided in Hong Kong before or after the establishment of the Hong Kong Special Administrative Region for a continuous period of 7 years or more, and persons of Chinese nationality born outside Hong Kong of such Chinese nationals;
—all other persons who have ordinarily resided in Hong Kong before or after the establishment of the Hong Kong Special Administrative Region for a continuous period of 7 years or more and who have taken Hong Kong as their place of permanent residence before or after the

establishment of the Hong Kong Special Administrative Region, and persons under 21 years of age who were born of such persons in Hong Kong before or after the establishment of the Hong Kong Special Administrative Region;
—any other persons who had the right of abode only in Hong Kong before the establishment of the Hong Kong Special Administrative Region.

The Central People's Government shall authorise the Hong Kong Special Administrative Region Government to issue, in accordance with the law, passports of the Hong Kong Special Administrative Region of the People's Republic of China to all Chinese nationals who hold permanent identity cards of the Hong Kong Special Administrative Region, and travel documents of the Hong Kong Special Administrative Region of the People's Republic of China to all other persons lawfully residing in the Hong Kong Special Administrative Region. The above passports and documents shall be valid for all states and regions and shall record the holder's right to return to the Hong Kong Special Administrative Region.

For the purpose of travelling to and from the Hong Kong Special Administrative Region, residents of the Hong Kong Special Administrative Region may use travel documents issued by the Hong Kong Special Administrative Region Government, or by other competent authorities of the People's Republic of China, or of other states. Holders of permanent identity cards of the Hong Kong Special Administrative Region may have this fact stated in their travel documents as evidence that the holders have the right of abode in the Hong Kong Special Administrative Region.

Entry into the Hong Kong Special Administrative Region of persons from other parts of China shall continue to be regulated in accordance with the present practice.

The Hong Kong Special Administrative Region Government may apply immigration controls on entry, stay in and departure from the Hong Kong Special Administrative Region by persons from foreign states and regions.

Unless restrained by law, holders of valid travel documents

shall be free to leave the Hong Kong Special Administrative Region without special authorisation.

The Central People's Government shall assist or authorise the Hong Kong Special Administrative Region Government to conclude visa abolition agreements with states or regions.

ANNEX II
SINO-BRITISH JOINT LIAISON GROUP

1.   In furtherance of their common aim and in order to ensure a smooth transfer of government in 1997, the Government of the People's Republic of China and the Government of the United Kingdom have agreed to continue their discussions in a friendly spirit and to develop the cooperative relationship which already exists between the two Governments over Hong Kong with a view to the effective implementation of the Joint Declaration.

2.   In order to meet the requirements for liaison, consultation and the exchange of information, the two Governments have agreed to set up a Joint Liaison Group.

3.   The functions of the Joint Liaison Group shall be:

> (a)   to conduct consultations on the implementation of the Joint Declaration;
> (b)   to discuss matters relating to the smooth transfer of government in 1997;
> (c)   to exchange information and conduct consultations on such subjects as may be agreed by the two sides.

Matters on which there is disagreement in the Joint Liaison Group shall be referred to the two Governments for solution through consultations.

4.   Matters for consideration during the first half of the period between the establishment of the Joint Liaison Group and 1 July 1997 shall include:

(a)   action to be taken by the two Governments to enable the Hong Kong Special Administrative Region to maintain its economic relations as a separate customs territory, and in particular to ensure the maintenance of Hong Kong's participation in the General Agreement on Tariffs and Trade, the Multifibre Arrangement and other international arrangements; and
(b)   action to be taken by the two Governments to ensure the continued application of international rights and obligations affecting Hong Kong.

5.   The two Governments have agreed that in the second half of the period between the establishment of the Joint Liaison Group and 1 July 1997 there will be need for closer cooperation, which will therefore be intensified during that period. Matters for consideration during this second period shall include:

(a)   procedures to be adopted for the smooth transition in 1997;
(b)   action to assist the Hong Kong Special Administrative Region to maintain and develop economic and cultural relations and conclude agreements on these matters with states, regions and relevant international organisations.

6.   The Joint Liaison Group shall be an organ for liaison and not an organ of power. It shall play no part in the administration of Hong Kong or the Hong Kong Special Administrative Region. Nor shall it have any supervisory role over that administration. The members and supporting staff of the Joint Liaison Group shall only conduct activities within the scope of the functions of the Joint Liaison Group.

7.   Each side shall designate a senior representative, who shall be of Ambassadorial rank, and four other members of the group. Each side may send up to 20 supporting staff.

8.   The Joint Liaison Group shall be established on the entry into force of the Joint Declaration. From 1 July 1988 the Joint Liaison Group shall have its principal base in Hong Kong.

The Joint Liaison Group shall continue its work until 1 January 2000.

9.   The Joint Liaison Group shall meet in Beijing, London and Hong Kong. It shall meet at least once in each of the three locations in each year. The venue for each meeting shall be agreed between the two sides.

10.   Members of the Joint Liaison Group shall enjoy diplomatic privileges and immunities as appropriate when in the three locations. Proceedings of the Joint Liaison Group shall remain confidential unless otherwise agreed between the two sides.

11.   The Joint Liaison Group may by agreement between the two sides decide to set up specialist sub-groups to deal with particular subjects requiring expert assistance.

12.   Meetings of the Joint Liaison Group and sub-groups may be attended by experts other than the members of the Joint Liaison Group. Each side shall determine the composition of its delegation to particular meetings of the Joint Liaison Group or sub-group in accordance with the subjects to be discussed and the venue chosen.

13.   The working procedures of the Joint Liaison Group shall be discussed and decided upon by the two sides within the guidelines laid down in this Annex.

ANNEX III
LAND LEASES

The Government of the United Kingdom and the Government of the People's Republic of China have agreed that, with effect from the entry into force of the Joint Declaration, land leases in Hong Kong and other related matters shall be dealt with in accordance with the following provisions:

1. All leases of land granted or decided upon before the entry into force of the Joint Declaration and those granted thereafter in accordance with paragraphs 2 or 3 of this Annex, and which extend beyond 30 June 1997, and all rights in relation to such leases shall continue to be recognised and protected under the law of the Hong Kong Special Administrative Region.

2. All leases of land granted by the British Hong Kong Government not containing a right of renewal that expire before 30 June 1997, except short term tenancies and leases for special purposes, may be extended if the lessee so wishes for a period expiring not later than 30 June 2047 without payment of an additional premium. An annual rent shall be charged from the date of extension equivalent to 3 per cent of the rateable value of the property at that date, adjusted in step with any changes in the rateable value thereafter. In the case of old schedule lots, village lots, small houses and similar rural holdings, where the property was on 30 June 1984 held by, or, in the case of small houses

granted after that date, the property is granted to, a person descended through the male line from a person who was in 1898 a resident of an established village in Hong Kong, the rent shall remain unchanged so long as the property is held by that person or by one of his lawful successors in the male line. Where leases of land not having a right of renewal expire after 30 June 1997, they shall be dealt with in accordance with the relevant land laws and policies of the Hong Kong Special Administrative Region.

3. From the entry into force of the Joint Declaration until 30 June 1997, new leases of land may be granted by the British Hong Kong Government for terms expiring not later than 30 June 2047. Such leases shall be granted at a premium and nominal rental until 30 June 1997, after which date they shall not require payment of an additional premium but an annual rent equivalent to 3 per cent of the rateable value of the property at that date, adjusted in step with changes in the rateable value thereafter, shall be charged.

4. The total amount of new land to be granted under paragraph 3 of this Annex shall be limited to 50 hectares a year (excluding land to be granted to the Hong Kong Housing Authority for public rental housing) from the entry into force of the Joint Declaration until 30 June 1997.

5. Modifications of the conditions specified in leases granted by the British Hong Kong Government may continue to be granted before 1 July 1997 at a premium equivalent to the difference between the value of the land under the previous conditions and its value under the modified conditions.

6. From the entry into force of the Joint Declaration until 30 June 1997, premium income obtained by the British Hong Kong Government from land transactions shall, after deduction of the average cost of land production, be shared equally between the British Hong Kong Government and the future Hong Kong Special Administrative Region Government. All the income obtained by the British Hong Kong Government, including the amount of the above-mentioned deduction, shall be put into the Capital Works Reserve Fund for the financing of land development and public works in Hong Kong. The Hong Kong Special Administrative Region Government's share of the pre-

mium income shall be deposited in banks incorporated in Hong Kong and shall not be drawn on except for the financing of land development and public works in Hong Kong in accordance with the provisions of paragraph 7 (d) of this Annex.

7. A Land Commission shall be established in Hong Kong immediately upon the entry into force of the Joint Declaration. The Land Commission shall be composed of an equal number of officials designated respectively by the Government of the United Kingdom and the Government of the People's Republic of China together with necessary supporting staff. The officials of the two sides shall be responsible to their respective governments. The Land Commission shall be dissolved on 30 June 1997.

The terms of reference of the Land Commission shall be:

(a) to conduct consultations on the implementation of this Annex;
(b) to monitor observance of the limit specified in paragraph 4 of this Annex, the amount of land granted to the Hong Kong Housing Authority for public rental housing, and the division and use of premium income referred to in paragraph 6 of this Annex;
(c) to consider and decide on proposals from the British Hong Kong Government for increasing the limit referred to in paragraph 4 of this Annex;
(d) to examine proposals for drawing on the Hong Kong Special Administrative Region Government's share of premium income referred to in paragraph 6 of this Annex and to make recommendations to the Chinese side for decision.

Matters on which there is disagreement in the Land Commission shall be referred to the Government of the United Kingdom and Government of the People's Republic of China for decision.

8. Specific details regarding the establishment of the Land Commission shall be finalised separately by the two sides through consultations.

MEMORANDA

(To Be Exchanged Between the Two Sides)

MEMORANDUM

In connection with the Joint Declaration of the Government of the United Kingdom of Great Britain and Northern Ireland and the Government of the People's Republic of China on the question of Hong Kong to be signed this day, the Government of the United Kingdom declares that, subject to the completion of the necessary amendments to the relevant United Kingdom legislation:

(a) All persons who on 30 June 1997 are, by virtue of a connection with Hong Kong, British Dependent Territories citizens (BDTCs) under the law in force in the United Kingdom will cease to be BDTCs with effect from 1 July 1997, but will be eligible to retain an appropriate status which, without conferring the right of abode in the United Kingdom, will entitle them to continue to use passports issued by the Government of the United Kingdom. This status will be acquired by such persons only if they hold or are included in such a British passport issued before 1 July 1997, except that eligible persons born on or after 1 January 1997 but before 1 July 1997 may obtain or be included in such a passport up to 31 December 1997.

(b) No person will acquire BDTC status on or after 1 July 1997 by virtue of a connection with Hong Kong. No person born on or after 1 July 1997 will acquire the status referred to as being appropriate in sub-paragraph (a).

(c) United Kingdom consular officials in the Hong Kong Special Administrative Region and elsewhere may renew and replace passports of persons mentioned in sub-paragraph (a) and may also issue them to persons, born before 1 July 1997 of such persons, who had previously been included in the passport of their parent.

(d) Those who have obtained or been included in passports issued by the Government of the United Kingdom under subparagraphs (a) and (c) will be entitled to receive, upon request, British consular services and protection when in third countries.

MEMORANDUM

The Government of the People's Republic of China has received the memorandum from the Government of the United Kingdom of Great Britain and Northern Ireland dated   1984.

Under the Nationality Law of the People's Republic of China, all Hong Kong Chinese compatriots, whether they are holders of the "British Dependent Territories citizens' Passport" or not, are Chinese nationals.

Taking account of the historical background of Hong Kong and its realities, the competent authorities of the Government of the People's Republic of China will, with effect from 1 July 1997, permit Chinese nationals in Hong Kong who were previously called "British Dependent Territories citizens" to use travel documents issued by the Government of the United Kingdom for the purpose of travelling to other states and regions.

The above Chinese nationals will not be entitled to British consular protection in the Hong Kong Special Administrative Region and other parts of the People's Republic of China on account of their holding the above-mentioned British travel documents.

Notes

1—THINKING ABOUT POLITICS

1. Carl Hempel, cited in Alan C. Isaak, *Scope and Methods of Political Science* (Homewood, III.: Dorsey Press, 1981), p. 171. Isaak provides a useful overview of the topics mentioned in this introduction.

2—HOW TO ANALYZE POLITICS

1. Imre Lakatos, *The Methodology of Scientific Research Programs*, vol. 1. (London: Cambridge University Press, 1978), p. 32.

2. Bruce Bueno de Mesquita, *The War Trap* (New Haven: Yale University Press, 1981); and Bruce Bueno de Mesquita, "The War Trap Revisited," *American Political Science Review* 79 (March 1985): 156–177.

3. Douglas Beck and Bruce Bueno de Mesquita, "Forecasting Policy Decisions: An Expected Utility Approach," in *Corporate Crisis Management*, ed. Steven Andriole (New York: Petrocelli Books, 1984).

4. The Mexican analysis reported here is based on studies done by Policon Corporation in conjunction with Data Resources Inc. exclusively using the model reported here. These studies are DRI/Policon, *Mexico* (November 19, 1982) and DRI/Policon, *Mexico: Can the Austerity Last?* (October 18, 1983).

5. Bruce Bueno de Mesquita, "Forecasting Policy Decisions: An

Expected Utility Approach to Post-Khomeini Iran," *PS* (Spring 1984): 226–36.

6. ABC News, Rochester, New York (October 1979).

7. Bruce Bueno de Mesquita, "Conflict Forecasting Project: Iran and Soviet Union Analysis," Defense Advanced Research Projects Agency (April 1982).

8. Bueno de Mesquita, "The War Trap Revisited."

9. Beck and Bueno de Mesquita, "Forecasting Policy Decisions: An Expected Utility Approach."

10. The analyses of the Philippines are based on studies done in conjunction with DRI/Policon, using the model presented in this book. These are available as part of the online computer service provided jointly by Data Resources Inc. and Policon Corporation. More recent analyses of the Philippines indicate a deteriorating situation.

11. Duncan Black, *Voting in Committees and Elections* (Cambridge: Cambridge University Press, 1958).

12. For a detailed discussion of this procedure, see Bueno de Mesquita, *The War Trap* and "The War Trap Revisited."

13. This concept of security is developed in detail in David Newman, "Security and Alliances: A Theoretical Study of Alliance Formation," a paper presented at the 1982 annual meeting of the International Studies Association.

14. Research in this area is being conducted by David Lalman and Bruce Bueno de Mesquita.

3—HONG KONG: A TEST CASE

1. The historical background leading up to the expiration of Britain's lease on the New Territories in 1997 and the major issues it raises are described in David Bonavia, *Hong Kong 1997* (Hong Kong: South China Morning Post, 1983).

2. For an excellent political history of the founding and early years of Hong Kong, see G. B. Endacott, *Government and People in Hong Kong* (Hong Kong: Hong Kong University Press, 1964).

3. Leo Goodstadt, "The Hong Kong Question," *Euromoney* (July 1983): 115.

4. Bonavia, *Hong Kong 1997*, p. 115.

5. *Financial Times*, May 10, 1984, p. 3.

6. This treatment of Hong Kong's political economy draws heavily from Alvin Rabushka, *Value for Money: The Hong Kong Budgetary Process* (Stanford: Hoover Press, 1976); and Alvin Rabushka, *Hong*

Kong: A Study in Economic Freedom (Chicago: University of Chicago Press, 1979). The first volume analyzes policymaking and budgetary practice within the Hong Kong government. The second presents a comprehensive treatment of politics and business in Hong Kong, showing the structure of the colony's free market economy and documenting its remarkable economic growth.

7. Bonavia, *Hong Kong 1997*, pp. 63−66.

8. Hong Kong, Census and Statistics Dept., *Estimates of Gross Domestic Product 1966 to 1983*, (Hong Kong, 1984) table 2, p. 8.

9. Rabushka, *Hong Kong: A Study in Economic Freedom*, pp. 43−82.

10. Rabushka, *Value for Money*.

11. S. C. Chow and G. F. Papanek, "Laissez-Faire, Growth and Equity—Hong Kong," *Economic Journal* 91, no. 362 (June 1981): 466−85.

12. These figures appear in *The 1982−83 Budget: Speech by the Financial Secretary, Moving the Second Reading of the Appropriation Bill, 1982* (February 24, 1982), para. 95, p. 39.

13. See Leo Goodstadt, "The Hong Kong Dollar," *Asian Banking* (June 1983): 62−67; and Leo Goodstadt, "Tugging the Currency Off the Reefs," *Asian Banking* (November 1983): 38−44. For a detailed treatment of this process by the architect of Hong Kong's linked rate see John Greenwood, "The Stabilization of the Hong Kong Dollar," *Asian Monetary Monitor* 7, no. 6 (November−December 1983): 9−37; and John Greenwood, "The Operation of the New Exchange Rate Mechanism," *Asian Monetary Monitor* 8, no. 1 (January−February 1984): 2−12.

14. Daily figures of the Hang Seng stock exchange index are published in the weekly edition of the *Far Eastern Economic Review*, a Hong Kong−based news magazine.

15. *The 1984−85 Budget: Speech by the Financial Secretary, Moving the Second Reading of the Appropriation Bill, 1984* (February 29, 1984), para. 13, p. 6.

16. *The Economist*, March 31, 1984, pp. 69−70; *The Wall Street Journal*, March 29, 1984, p. 30.

17. *The Wall Street Journal*, March 29, 1984, p. 30.

18. Reported in Hong Kong Government Information Services, "This Week in Hong Kong," April 24, 1984.

19. Derived from *Hong Kong Monthly Digest of Statistics* (January 1984), tables 5.4 and 5.5, pp. 24−25. See also A. J. Youngson, ed., *China and Hong Kong: The Economic Nexus* (Hong Kong: Oxford University Press, 1983).

20. Mary Lee, "A Backdoor to Britain," *Far Eastern Economic Review*, May 5, 1983, p. 14.

21. Goodstadt, "The Hong Kong Question," p. 113. For the viewpoints of local critics see H. K. Lamb, *A Date with Fate* (Hong Kong: Lincoln Green, 1984).

22. *The Economist*, May 19, 1984, pp. 13–14.

23. Bonavia, *Hong Kong 1997*, pp. 99–101.

24. Philip Bowring and Teresa Ma, "Promises, Promises," *Far Eastern Economic Review*, May 17, 1984, pp. 18–19.

25. Bonavia, *Hong Kong 1997*, pp. 121–22.

26. *Financial Times*, May 10, 1984.

27. Rabushka, *Value for Money*, pp. 12–37.

28. Derek Davies, "A Leap into the Dark," *Far Eastern Economic Review*, May 3, 1984, p. 16.

29. *The Wall Street Journal*, May 29, 1984, p. 30.

30. Frank Ching, "Hong Kong's Trading Partners are Wary, Too," *The Wall Street Journal*, January 30, 1984, p. 27.

6—THE POST-AGREEMENT ADMINISTRATION OF HONG KONG

1. Figures 6.4, 6.5, and 6.11 are not absolutely faithful reproductions of the spatial array of the data. Slight imprecisions have been introduced because of the difficulties associated with clear graphic display when groups are close together.

Index